WELL ON YOUR WAY

Looking after yourself in the great outdoors

Pat and Hazel Constance

SIGMA Leisure

Published by Sigma Leisure – an imprint of
Sigma Press, 1 South Oak Lane, Wilmslow, Cheshire SK9 6AR, England.

British Library Cataloguing in Publication Data
A CIP record for this book is available from the British Library.

ISBN: 1-85058-409-5

Typesetting and Design by: Sigma Press, Wilmslow, Cheshire.

Maps: Jeremy Semmens

Cover photograph: Ascending Bush Howe, The Howgills *(Terry Marsh)*

Cover Design: The Agency, Wilmslow

Printed by: Manchester Free Press

PREFACE

Throughout our lives, both of us have enjoyed much of our free time walking, cycling and camping, either alone, together, or in earlier years with our two daughters. In Pat's case some of his earliest memories at the tender age of five are of studying maps with his father prior to setting out on a bus from Exeter into the countryside for a walk with his parents and older brother. The ultimate aim was the promised walks on 'the Moors' – his parents had spent many days walking all over Dartmoor some eighty years ago.

We first met on our way to join a group of Rover Scouts and Ranger Guides for a very muddy walk in Surrey in January 1951 – an annual event which culminated in our marriage. Since then we have continued our active interest in the outdoors, both in this country and overseas.

In earlier times folk living in or near the country seemed to be able to take the weather in their stride, as it were, but nowadays the majority of the population lives a much more sheltered existence. As a consequence, people seem much less able to withstand the rigours of going out at all times of the year in all weathers. Nevertheless, with the development of new equipment, especially clothing, far more people today are going out all the year round for pleasure.

We believe that the average person or family out to enjoy a pleasant walk or ride in the country is just as likely to run into problems as are the "hard ones" who are probably well prepared and equipped to cope with difficult situations when pushing themselves to the limit in extreme conditions.

We have found that a little preparation beforehand can avoid many of the problems which can crop up at any time in the great outdoors. We hope that this book will be a useful companion to SIGMA's walking and cycling guides, and so encourage and help day and weekend walkers and cyclists to stay on course and enjoy their journeys.

In conclusion, we must thank those who have offered advice or helped us in other ways during the preparation of this book, not least to Graham Beech of Sigma Press for his patience. We are indebted to Terry Marsh, who supplied the cover photograph, and to Silva (UK) Ltd who gave us permission to use some of their material. Thanks also to Tim Wish, of Linsports, Lincoln, for allowing us to take photographs in his shop, to Clive Green and his family, and to Chris Juden of the Cyclists' Touring Club, Gill Gaskin of Yoredale

Weatherwear, Ian Gibson of Calange, and Derek Wood of the Camping and Caravanning Club's Mountain Activity Section for the use of their photographs.

Pat and Hazel Constance

Contents

INTRODUCTION

GETTING STARTED

Walking is the most popular outdoor activity in the U.K. and, since the advent of the 'mountain bike', cycling must come a pretty close second.

Walking is for Everyone

The joy of walking is that you need very little equipment to get started – some would say you need *no* special equipment – and virtually everyone from the smallest babe to the ageing grandparent can enjoy the activity. You can go for a short stroll in your local town or village or go to a local beauty spot, in which case it is unlikely you'll need a map to help you find the way, but obviously you will need to make some preparations. For all but the shortest walk you may like to take some kind of snack with you to keep the wolf from the door, even if it is only a two hour morning or afternoon outing. In warm weather some cash to enable you to buy drinks or an ice-cream will be welcome, similarly a hot drink to keep out the cold at other times of the year.

Walking is for everyone! (Hazel Constance)

Plan for the Children

If you are taking children with you, you might like to take something to keep them occupied, such as an 'I spy in the Countryside' book, or even a small ball or skipping rope to cater for the odd outburst of energy! Babies and toddlers often need to be carried, at least for part of the way, and special child carriers, though not by any means cheap, can help ease the burden. Most 'buggies' are light enough to be lifted over stiles when necessary, and can cope well with grass and unmade, but firm tracks. Children who are too big to be carried can often be jollied along by other means. We devote a whole chapter to suggesting ways of keeping your children safe and well in the countryside.

Cycling: a Family Activity

Cycling, too, can be enjoyed by all the family, with many routes along quiet country lanes, roads and bridleways far from the noise and rush of traffic. By setting an easy pace and using some of the readily available aids for carrying very small children too young to cycle on their own, this can be a real family affair. At the other end of the scale, very low geared machines can help those less active ones amongst us to cope with hills, and even small electric motors can now be obtained to assist the less able to pedal their way along peaceful lanes without polluting the atmosphere! Cycles should be in good mechanical condition and properly equipped before setting out.

Summer walking, near Bolton Castle (Derek Wood)

Plan in Advance

Walks or rides in less familiar surroundings will require a little advanced planning to help you decide where to go, and some kind of a map or guide book will be needed to help you find your way. Whether it be walking in the Peak District or Lake District, the Chilterns or Wales, or simply a walk from one of the pubs in your home county, Sigma Leisure will have a guide book for you and there are also Sigma guides describing cycle runs. In this book we hope to explain how you can supplement those and other guide books with additional information about your route and surroundings. You may even like to plan your own routes to fit in with your own special interests. This requires the use of maps and some idea of the time it will take to cover the distance you want to go.

Comfort and Protection

Comfortable clothing and suitable footwear are just as important for cyclists as for walkers. Because of the vagaries of our proverbial British weather you'll want at least a light waterproof, and possibly an extra jersey or light fleece jacket. In the following chapters we offer advice on such matters to cover the whole range of experience, from short summer walks to extended walking and cycling trips in more rugged country.

Further afield

Pre-planning is even more important if you intend extending your journey over several days. Accomodation and its pros and cons are dealt with in a special chapter, which includes advice on such matters as Youth Hostelling with children, backpacking and cycle camping. Advice is also offered on safety if you venture into hilly country. You may try our ideas on predicting the weather, but even the experts get it wrong sometimes, so you need to know what to do if caught out. Getting lost is the last thing you want to do, so we advise how to avoid such a situation.

Other Essentials

Whether you walk or ride, you are the engine and food is your fuel, so that is something to think about. Some tips on being prepared for the odd minor cuts and scratches, nettle stings or insect bites, with suggestions for a simple first aid kit, including insect repellent, are given in Chapter Six. First aid for the bike should not be forgotten, either.

Some means of carrying all these bits and pieces will be needed, so ideas on the most comfortable and safest ways of doing so are explained in some detail.

A winter ramble with a group of friends

Flexibility

Walks or cycle rides can begin at your own front door, at whatever time you decide on. You can wait for the weather to be kind, or you can choose to go out on a dull rainy day. You might have to modify your timing to allow for public transport to get to a more distant starting point, but flexibility is the key-word for maximum enjoyment of both such outings. Once you get immersed in the art of walking or cycling for pleasure, you can plan longer trips, staying away from home for a night or more and making use of the various types of accomodation we describe.

Be Aware – and Be Prepared

Whatever you choose to do, there are many organisations who can help, and many publications which cater for the walker or cyclist. In our last chapter we give details of a number of these, together with some useful check lists and addresses of firms who can supply clothing or equipment. Some hints on looking after your gear are given so you can be ready and prepared to go off at any time.

In an early chapter we explain the position regarding access to the countryside. A summary of the generally accepted rules governing behaviour in the countryside, both for walkers and cyclists, together with some useful guidelines for those venturing into the hills, are set out in this last chapter, and we hope that by adhering to these codes, readers will not only enjoy their own outings, but will maintain the countryside in good shape for those who follow.

We have enjoyed these and similar activities for many years, enabling us to travel and see the countryside in all its variety of scenery and weather. We have drawn on our own experiences to produce this book, which we hope will be a companion to the many Sigma walking and cycling guides which are available, giving more detailed general information about equipment, navigation and safety than can possibly be included in any single walking or cycling guide. Perhaps we should have called it a guide to the guides. We hope that some of the things we have learned over the years will help you to enjoy your outings in the countryside and to go 'well on your way'.

CHAPTER ONE

GOING ON FOOT

Clothing and Footwear

Initially you will need to spend very little on specialised clothing, particularly if you are planning to walk in lowland countryside in fine weather. Comfortable underwear, a tee-shirt or polo shirt, and comfortable slacks or shorts are quite adequate, so long as you remember to carry a spare pullover and a lightweight waterproof. Don't wear jeans as they can chafe the legs and take ages to dry when they get wet (as they will). Wet jeans can be very uncomfortable, especially in cold wet weather with a breeze blowing, and you can get very chilled. Once you start walking on a regular basis in more variable weather conditions and for longer walks, you will probably find that 'ordinary' clothes are not quite as comfortable as you thought they would be! Cotton shirts can become very damp with perspiration after only the slightest exertion, and when you stop for a break you'll find yourself feeling somewhat chilled around the waistline. If it rains and you have had to put on your waterproof, condensation can build up inside with the same results. In cold weather an ordinary pullover may not be sufficient to keep you warm and comfortable, and you will need to think of an alternative. Ordinary low-heeled shoes or trainers may initially be quite satisfactory, but they need to be well broken in and comfortable. Socks should preferably have a loop-stitched inner along the sole and heel for extra absorbency and comfort; never wear a new pair of socks without having first washed them, as they are often, initially, quite hard on the feet and could cause rubbing. It may seem obvious, but never wear socks which have been heavily darned or which have holes in them! Once you get onto stony tracks or rough ground on longer walks you will soon realise why seasoned walkers wear specially made walking shoes or boots. It is also easy to put your foot into an unseen rabbit hole and twist your ankle, another good reason for examining your footwear.

A hole in your pocket

Buying good outdoor clothing can make an appreciable hole in your pocket but money well spent will be a good investment. What you can afford and what you need will depend on where you are going and when. The clothing required for a winter's day walk in freezing conditions will be different from that required for a family walk in an English country lane in summer time.

Layers are best

So, what should you be looking for when buying clothes for walking ? First of all, let's look at the principles of dressing comfortably for the outdoors which allow you to maintain your body at an even temperature and give maximum protection from the elements. Walking is an activity which produces body heat, but at the same time, the elements (wind and/or rain) can rapidly cool the body. You therefore need to be able to adjust your clothing to allow for these effects, hence the 'layer principle'. Next to the skin try to use underwear which will not cause chilling and will keep you comfortable, followed by clothes which keep you warm, and a top layer to provide protection against wind and rain. Whatever the weather and no matter where you are going, bear this principle in mind and you will not go far wrong.

Next to the skin

Let us begin with the unmentionable - underwear! What you wear next to your skin will determine how comfortable you are. All underwear needs to be reasonably thin, stretchy, and comfortable. As we've already said, cotton fibres soak up perspiration but do not dry quickly so chilling can occur. Synthetics are better because, unlike cotton, they will wick away perspiration from your skin and dry quicker. The best garments are those made from these 'wicking' fabrics, which will allow any moisture to be transported through the fibres to the outer surface of the garment. The inner surface remains dry, as does the body, thus preventing chilling when activity ceases. These wicking garments are popularly known as 'thermals' and are often associated with winter underwear. However, they can be used at any time of the year, and it is possible to obtain underwear for both sexes, also tee-shirts, made from similar materials which are more suitable for summer use. The thing to do is to read the labels in the garments in your high street store. Garments which include a high proportion of polyester, or are made entirely from it, are ideal, as they do not absorb dampness, allow moisture to wick along the fibres, and dry quickly. Some polyester fibres, such as Thermax, are specially constructed or treated to improve their insulation and wicking properties. Garments made from these materials will be more expensive than those found in high street stores but are worth seeking as they are mostly suitable for year-round use.

Coolmax is another brand of polyester fibre which has been specially developed for warm climates and summer use.

Polypropylene garments are very efficient at wicking away moisture, but they do tend to absorb body odours, making them unpleasant in warm weather. Chlorofibre and Rhovyl are other man-made fibres which have very efficient wicking properties, and tend to absorb less odour. Damart, a mail-order company with a number of high street shops, markets a wide range of thermal underwear for men, women and children using Chlorofibre. Lightweight polyester fleece garments, although principally designed for 'mid-wear', are ideal as underwear in colder conditions. Wool and silk are both good insulators. Silk is particularly comfortable in summer time, whilst wool soaks up moisture easily, and can generate heat when wet, reducing the risk of chilling. Whatever garment you buy, make sure it has sufficient stretch to enable ease of putting on and to give a comfortable fit.

Well protected against the elements

Midwear

Anything not classed as underwear or waterproof shell clothing is included in this category. Your choice will be dependant on conditions of use, but you will be able to regulate your body temperature by removing or adding layers as necessary. The best garments will be lightweight, offering good warmth value when dry or wet, and allowing perspiration vapour through to the outside. Fleece is ideal because it is available in different weights to suit individual requirements. It is made from knitted or woven polyester fibres and is exceptionally versatile, some fleeces having a high degree of wind resistance. It can be made into single or double faced cloths, and may be brushed on one or both sides. Fleeces are used for jackets, sweaters and trousers, most having good stretch properties. They are comfortable to wear, because the polyester fibres wick moisture away from the body. Wool shirts still have their devotees, but most people now choose fleece. One great advantage of many fleece garments is that they can be obtained with compatible zips so that you can fasten them into a waterproof jacket as a warm lining. These are known as 'interactive' garments.

Extra insulation in the form of wind-shirts or windproof shells can be worn over the fleece, avoiding the use of waterproofs for wind protection. Pertex, a light-weight tightly woven nylon fabric, can be used in place of cotton or polycotton for windshirts, its advantage being that it is very efficient at wicking away water by capillary action. Most microfibre fabrics are also windproof and water repellant and can be used for the same purpose.

Many walkers like to wear a windproof jacket, or even an old fashioned pull-on anorak, and these are often made from polycotton fabrics or 100% cotton, such as Ventile. The latter fabric, developed during World War II for survival suits for airmen, is a closely woven, wind tight fabric which will also keep out quite a fair degree of rain, but it gets very heavy when wet and takes a fair time to dry. Whatever is chosen, jacket or anorak, should have plenty of usable pockets and preferably a hood which can be tucked away in the collar.

Some manufacturers now produce excellent 'multi-purpose' outer garments which are windproof and waterproof, breathable, and are of very smart appearance. These have a microfibre fabric or polycotton shell, with a micro-liner consisting of a waterproof, breathable membrane laminated to a very lightweight lining. They can be worn anywhere from the High Street to HIGH STREET, but they do not come cheap. In very cold weather an insulated jacket or body-warmer may be needed. Materials designed to trap air, the best insulation there is, are 'sandwiched' between an outer and inner layer of tightly woven fabric to keep the air in place. Down, which is the lightest and most efficient of these materials, packs into a small space, but it is expensive and useless when wet. Modern synthetic fillings, on the other hand, are light-weight, warm and resistant to damp, making them particularly suitable for insulated clothing. Many are made from polyester micro-fibres, and the spaces created around these fibres during the construction of the wadding provide an enormous surface area to trap the air. In all except the most extreme conditions, good synthetic fillings are preferable for use in garments.

Most walkers of both sexes prefer to wear trousers for walking. There are many good brands of polyester/cotton 'action' trousers, with plenty of zipped pockets, which are ideal. Some are available with thermal linings for winter use, but all are made from tightly woven cloth which keeps out the wind and dries quickly when wet. Both men's and ladies fittings are available. Shorts, and even culottes for ladies, are available in the same fabrics for use in warm weather. An alternative favoured by some are 'tracksters', comfortable trousers made from polyester jersey fabric which also dry quickly when wet and are very comfortable to wear. Some walkers prefer breeches, made either from wool, moleskin, or one of the modern synthetic stretch fabrics. They are certainly comfortable, and when walking through long grass you are not plagued by wet trousers flapping round your ankles! They give a great sense of freedom, and in wet weather, worn with a long cagoule and a decent pair of gaiters, you don't have to worry about overtrousers. There is also the advantage that they are easily and cheaply made from old trousers, cut off below the knees!

Keeping out the wet

A waterproof shell garment, which is also windproof, is essential for every walker. Most will prefer a jacket to an 'over-the-head' smock. Well designed waterproofs have a double-ended front zip, protected by a storm flap to prevent rain driving through the teeth. A map pocket which can be reached from under the protective flap without undoing the front zip is most useful. The garment will zip high into the neckline, and will usually have two large skirt pockets. A hood, either attached to the neckline or tucked away under the collar, should fit closely around the face, secured with adjustable drawcords. A small peak at the front is very useful, especially if you wear spectacles. Detachable hoods can be a nuisance as they have to be carried in a pocket and are often difficult to put in place without removing the jacket. They are also very easily lost! Sleeves should be well cut and cuffs should be easily adjustable, both for keeping out driving rain and for ventilation.

The choice lies between 'non-breathables' and 'breathables'. Most cheaper waterproofs have a polyurethane coating which is applied to a base material - usually nylon. Both the coating and the base cloth may be available in different weights, so it is possible to get an ultra-light garment with a good thickness of proofing, which is ideal if you need something which will fold up small yet give reasonable protection. Quality manufacturers will apply several thin coatings to the base fabric, giving a more efficient proofing, and will tape the seams to prevent rain seepage through the garment at its most vulnerable points. Condensation can be a problem, and it is because of this that the 'Breathables' have been developed.

Breathable fabrics allow moisture vapour generated by the body to escape to the outside. They can be classified into two distinct types - microporous and hydrophilic. Microporous fabrics incorporate coatings or membranes in their structure containing millions of microscopic pores. These allow water vapour molecules from the wearer's body to pass from inside the fabric to the outer surface, but prevent droplets of rain water from passing through in the opposite direction. The pores can become clogged with mud and other dirt, so the fabrics must be washed frequently. Typical examples of this type of fabric include Gore-Tex, which is a membrane that is normally laminated to the shell fabric or lining, and Texapore, one of a number of microporous coatings which can be applied to the inside of the shell fabric. Hydrophilic coatings and membranes make use of certain polymers which attract water vapour molecules and allow them to pass through, whilst presenting an impermeable layer to water droplets. With this system there is no problem with dirt clogging the pores. Again there are two methods of applying the proofing. Sympatex is a hydrophilic membrane which can be laminated to a shell fabric or lining. Coatings made from a modified polyurethane can be applied to base fabrics. The coatings can be specially formulated to suit garment manufacturers' specific requirements, hence the large number of different brands available. Hydrophilic coated fabrics include Cascade, Helly-Tech, Hydrodry and VTX. The exterior surface of most 'breathables' is normally treated with a water-repellant treatment, which may eventually wear off. However, the problem is easily remedied by treating the outer surface with one of the specialist water-repellant treatments now available.

There can be no guarantee that a breathable garment will always be condensation-free. The principle by which breathables work is that the temperature, pressure and humidity inside the garment must be higher than that outside. If the surrounding humidity is very high your breathable garment will not breathe very well! Those who perspire freely may find that they produce water vapour at a rate greater than the fabric can dissipate, or the surrounding atmosphere can absorb, so condensation could occur. A combination of any of the above factors may produce dampness on the inside of your waterproof garment, but this does not mean that it is leaking.

The extremities

Before leaving the subject of clothing, remember your head, hands and feet. Thirty per cent of your body heat is lost through your head, so it's important to carry some kind of warm headwear in cold weather. You may not normally consider wearing a hat, even in winter, when in town, but in the open countryside, and even on quite low hills you can feel the wind and chill quickly. A simple bobble hat or a balaclava which can be rolled up at the bottom can make all the difference. There are now lots of colourful fleece headbands and hats of various kinds in the shops, and these are very cosy. In hot, sunny weather a cotton sun hat is useful to protect your head and the back of your neck from the sun. You will need gloves or mitts in cold weather, as well as warm, comfortable socks to wear inside your boots or shoes.

Dressing for the climate

The climate of the area where you are going walking will determine to some extent the type of clothing you wear. If you are out in the cold, damp conditions of an English winter you will need underwear which will wick away any perspiration which you generate, a good warm fleece mid-layer, and a waterproof to keep you dry. For gentle summer walks in mild weather, you can wear cotton underwear, a cotton or polycotton shirt or T-shirt, and polycotton shorts or trousers, taking a lightweight waterproof with you if the weather looks a little uncertain. Of course, for an afternoon walk during a hot sunny spell you can dispense with the waterproof, but on day long walks we reckon to carry one, even if it's only to keep the odd thundery shower away! On longer walks in hilly country, whatever the time of year, you'll need similar clothing to that required for winter walks, plus possibly a windshirt and a better waterproof.

On your feet

Boots or shoes? a wide choice

Comfortable boots or shoes are a must, otherwise you will end up with sore feet or blisters and you could even become a danger to yourself or, worse still, others who might have to turn out to rescue you. However, the wide choice available can lead to confusion; knowing what is required is half the battle, and it is worth seeking out specialist footwear which will improve your comfort and safety. Don't waste money on boots which are over-specified for the walking you have in mind; in other words, do not buy a pair of heavy duty mountain boots if you only intend walking on country lanes, where a pair of shoes will be perfectly adequate!

Before you even set out to buy a pair of boots, study the catalogues; most manufacturers will be happy to send you theirs, together with the name of your nearest retailer. Only you know what type of walking you are going to do; if it will be lowland walking in summer then light-weight boots or, in many cases, shoes will suffice. For walking in more rugged conditions, a good 'general' walking boot, which will give your ankles proper support, will serve you well. There is no need for heavy boots, which in any case have a detrimental effect on the environment. Modern soles are designed to do as little harm as possible to the ground. The sole of your boot is your contact with the ground, and a good tread, like that on a car tyre, will generally give a good grip, but watch out on wet ground. Most boots are made from leather or suede, and are available with different soles to suit many purposes. If you prefer very light footwear, fabric boots might be sufficient; but remember that they are not waterproof, unless a waterproof membrane is incorporated in the construction. You can, of course, treat them with a proprietary waterproofing compound, such as Texnik from Nikwax, or G-Sport from Grangers, or you could use some of the waterproof socks which are now on the market. Essentially, these are made from a breathable, waterproof membrane, and you wear them over ordinary socks. As with ordinary socks, you should ensure that they fit properly. A stitched 'bellows' tongue in the boots will help greatly in keeping out water when walking in wet grass or boggy terrain, and a padded ankle cuff can aid comfort. Most modern walking boots come with removable footbeds or insoles, allowing greater flexibility of fit. They are most comfortable to wear and give excellent support to the arch of the foot as well as allowing a better fit around the heel. They are also available separately from many good boot retailers.

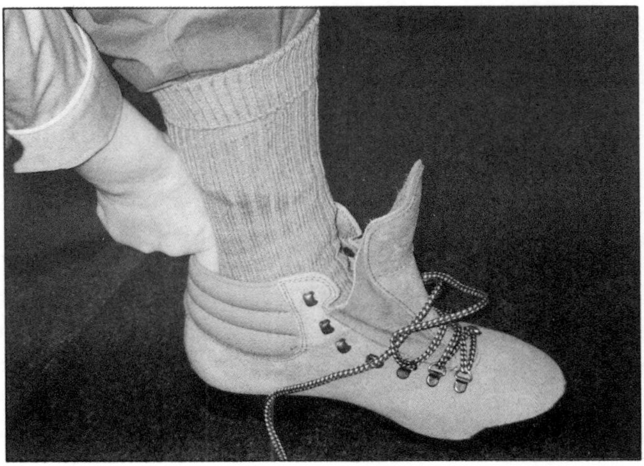

Trying on boots - you should just be able to get your finger down behind your heel

Fitting

Whatever footwear you choose, it needs to fit properly. When you go to buy your boots or shoes, take with you the socks you intend to wear when walking. As we've already said elsewhere, good loop-stitched socks are best; these can be made from cotton or synthetic mixtures, although most walkers will prefer those made from wool mixture. Never rush in to buy boots at the last minute! Take your time and try on several pairs until you are certain you will be comfortable; and if you are not sure about their comfort, then don't buy until you have had a chance to try other boots elsewhere. Some of the better quality boots will be available in a choice of width fittings, and if you have particularly broad or narrow feet, then tell the shop assistant, so that he does not waste his time bringing you boots which will not fit.

Do not be tempted to get a boot several sizes larger than you normally need to get the correct width fitting; a boot that is too long will not be comfortable, and after some use you will find that the leather will stretch and your foot will not be properly supported. When you try on a pair of boots or shoes, push your foot forward into the boot until it can go no further, then slide your index finger down behind your heel. There should just be room for your finger, and your boot should be about the right fit. Tighten the laces so that they are looser at the toes than at the ankle. Your heel should be held firmly and you should not be able to move it about, but you should be able to wriggle your toes. Make sure that the ankle cuff is comfortable and is not catching your ankle bone in the wrong place; if it is, the style is wrong for your shape of foot. Walk around the shop on a carpeted floor and make sure your feet feel comfortable. A good way of checking that there is no superfluous movement is to kick the toe of the boot against a carpeted stair riser, but you might not be able to do this in the shop. Ask if you can take the boots to wear around the house to ensure they are comfortable, and change them if you find they are not. Most shops are prepared for you to do this with expensive boots, but don't expect them to change them if you have marked them in any way or worn them outside! If you live miles away from a good boot retailer, and have no alternative, buy from a reliable mail order company prepared to take the boots back if they do not fit properly. Here again, don't expect them to take them back if you have marked them or worn them outside.

Breaking in

With the advent of softer leathers and fabric boots, this is not the problem it used to be, but you will still need to get used to wearing them before embarking on a long trek. Short walks near home are the best, and most enjoyable way of doing this job, making the walks progressively longer until you are well used to the boots. If you feel a 'hot spot' - a sure sign of a blister beginning to form, change into your normal footwear and let your feet recover before having another go. You should not get blisters if you have taken the trouble to fit your boots as we have suggested, but if you are prone to sore feet treat them in the old-fashioned way by rubbing the soles and heels with surgical spirit to harden the skin, powdering afterwards when the skin is dry with good quality talcum powder. There are also special protective plasters which can be used to cushion vulnerable spots.

Keeping out the wet

Gaiters are available from most outdoor shops, ranging from simple zipped waterproof tubes to expensive models made from breathable fabric. Others are specifically made to fit over the complete walking boot, with a special rubber rand to hold them in place. These have a front zip and can be attached to the boots before you put them on. All gaiters cover the top part of the boot, thus preventing moisture penetrating through the lacing holes, always a vulnerable point, especially if your boots are the inexpensive type without a bellows tongue. Gaiters are also useful for preventing loose twigs or small stones from getting into the tops of your boots.

Not just clothes!

Walkers need more than good clothes and footwear. They need to carry their food and a drink, or the means of making one, as well as spare clothes, and they will require something in which to pack it all.

A stove and pan?

In colder weather, to make hot soup or a piping hot drink requires either a stove and pan, or an insulated flask. For some there is nothing so good as a freshly made brew, but you have to weigh up the pros and cons. In the first place, you have to carry some water to boil for the drink or soup, but if you choose carefully your pan, stove and container of fuel could weigh less than one or two flasks of hot liquid. It's entirely up to you.

Most modern lightweight stoves weigh very little and pack up small. For convenience on shorter walks, gas in resealable disposable cartridges is ideal. Choose either a small burner which screws directly onto the cartridge when in use, or a folding unit with supporting legs and pan supports which connects to the cartridge through a short hose. This latter type has the advantage that it is more stable on the ground. Both types fold up very small for packing. We suggest using a separate windshield, which again can be a folding type taking very little space when packed. Use a light aluminium pan with lid and detachable handle, into which the stove may be packed after wrapping it in a piece of cloth or kitchen roll to prevent rattles and scratching of the metal. For added safety when using a stove screwed onto the gas cartridge, a rubber stabilising base can be used, or the cartridge can be secured by tent pegs to the ground. We do not recommend using stoves with pierceable cartridges which cannot be removed until empty, as they are bulkier to pack and run the risk of the valve being turned on accidentally in your rucksack.

A stove and a pan? Tiny Epigas 'Micro' stove is ideal for carrying on a day out.

A lot of walkers still prefer the favourite flask of tea or coffee. Unbreakable stainless steel flasks, although very expensive and rather heavy, are worth considering. Trip over a stone and land heavily, and an ordinary glass vacuum flask could break, leaving you with no drink. Carrying bottles of any liquid in a rucksack always means there is a risk of spillage, so it is sensible to put bottles or flasks inside plastic bags before packing them.

Packing your needs

It does not matter how short a distance you will be walking, the fact remains that to carry your needs in a carrier bag in your hand is not conducive to your comfort!

It is far more comfortable for a walker to carry his needs on his back than anywhere else. Do not choose a day sack that is too small, as there is nothing worse than carrying a sack stuffed to look like a football! It will be uncomfortable, and you will have no room for any 'extras' you might find or buy on your walk. Rucksack capacity is measured in litres, although when you look at the various sacks which are nominally the same size, the actual measurements vary surprisingly! We suggest that the minimum practical size for a daysack, for an adult, is 25 or 30 litres; most packs in this size range have a front pocket or two side ones, as well as the main compartment. Many may prefer a larger 45 litre pack, especially if they are having to carry extra gear for younger members of their family, but such a sack is also useful for extended trips, and avoids having to buy two. A 20 litre sack is ideal for a child, and can also be used daily for school!

Fitting your pack

A rucksack will not be comfortable if it does not fit properly. This applies particularly when carrying large loads, but even a badly fitting day sack can cause problems. The shoulder slings need to be adjustable, and preferably slightly shaped and padded, so that they feel comfortable over the shoulders. A waist strap is useful to prevent the sack from swinging about on your back. A padded back, preferably made from a fabric which will not absorb perspiration, will be more comfortable than a non-padded back, through which you will feel every edge of your sandwich box, flask, etc. If you have a long back, try and get a sack which is long and narrow, rather than short and broad, or choose a slightly larger sack. These, with a capacity of more than 40 litres, will usually have a hip belt transferring the weight from your shoulders to your hips, making the carrying easier and more comfortable.

When your pack is being worn, the fixing point of the shoulder slings should be between the tops of your shoulder blades for maximum comfort. Some sacks, even quite small ones, have a chest strap, which is particularly useful if you have narrow shoulders as it stops the straps from slipping off.

CHAPTER TWO

GOING BY BIKE

Clothing and footwear for cyclists

Much of what we have said concerning walkers in Chapter One will also apply to cyclists, and to begin with you will not need anything special in the way of equipment. Comfortable underwear is essential of course, to which a tee-shirt or track top and comfortable shorts or light slacks may be added. Some prefer the popular stretch shorts or leggings, which are currently very fashionable to wear for all activities by modern day youth. These are available in many chain stores and even on market stalls. This type of clothing is fine if you are going at a leisurely pace, although it is important to make sure there are no raised seams to chafe the legs inside the thighs, and of course shorts must not be too tight. Many cyclists do not use waterproofs unless the weather is very wet indeed. On a bike, wet clothing will dry quickly when the rain stops, but a lot of condensation can build up under waterproofs, which is why some don't bother! Track mitts, obtainable from branches of Halfords and specialist cycle shops, are worth getting from the start. They need not cost much, but will cushion your hands and prevent them from getting sore.

Once you start doing a lot of cycling, you may find that everyday clothes are not quite right for your needs and you might want to think of more specialist cycle clothing.

A good investment

Buying good cycle clothing can also make a hole in your pocket, but again by choosing wisely you make a good investment. What you can afford and what you need will depend on where you are going and when. The clothing required for a long winter ride will be different from that required for a summer one, and will also depend to a certain extent on the type of country you are cycling through. The Fens, for example, may be flat, but there is little shelter and you will encounter a lot of wind and much unpleasantness in heavy rain. The sheltered country lanes of Surrey are different, although you'll have to cope with a few steep gradients.

Layers are best

The best way of dressing is to use the 'layer' principle, already described in Chapter One, which allows you to maintain your body at an even temperature and give maximum protection from the elements. Cycling is an activity which generates a great deal more body heat than walking, and at the same time, the elements (wind and/or rain) have a greater cooling effect because you are moving at a greater speed than a walker. The need to allow the body to breathe, and the ability of the clothing to absorb perspiration is important, as is the need to provide protection from the sun and wind. You have to be able to adjust your clothing to allow for these effects, hence the 'layer principle'. Next to the skin you require underwear which will not cause chilling and will keep you comfortable, followed by a second layer so that you can adjust the clothes to suit your body temperature. This second layer can vary according to season, from a light polyester cycling jersey to a thick fleece top. A top layer to provide protection against both wind and rain is necessary in Great Britain because of the vagaries of the climate. Whatever the weather and no matter where you are going, bear this principle in mind and you will not go far wrong.

Next to the skin

As a cyclist, it is very important to wear comfortable underwear. It goes without saying that anything which rubs or chafes your anatomy in that area which is in contact with your saddle will cause you misery! Because cotton fibres soak up perspiration but do not dry quickly, chilling can occur because of the headwind you create when riding. In hot weather, a cotton T-shirt may seem a godsend to a hot cyclist, but in reality the synthetics are far better. These wick away perspiration from your skin, dry quicker, and prevent the body from becoming chilled when activity ceases. Synthetic garments are available in various weights, so there is a good choice available to suit your needs. Many cyclists choose to wear polypropylene tops, which may be obtained with both long and short sleeves, and are very stretchy and comfortable.

Midwear

Some will choose to wear the polypropylene tops mentioned above in place of a jersey, but there are disadvantages to this, not least the lack of pockets.

Cycling jerseys are normally made from knitted polyester and have pockets at the back to enable you to reach for your map, handkerchief, Mars Bar, etc, when riding. They are also long in the back, thus preventing chilling when you are in a bent-over riding position. (It is very easy, when leaning forward on a bike, to find your clothing riding up and exposing the lumbar regions to chill winds.) The polyester fibres have low water absorption properties, making them comfortable to wear. Stretch fabrics are used a lot in cycle clothing, because loose garments are a nuisance on a bike. The only exception to this rule is in very hot weather, when a loose cotton shirt with long sleeves, to protect arms from the sun, will be found to be the most comfortable. Any breeze generated by the movement of the cycle will cause the shirt to blow about, thus helping to cool the body. Stretch fabrics contain fibres such as elastane, which, combined with polyester and other fibres make a strong, stretchable fabric which has low water absorption and good windproof properties and is fast-drying. Some cycling jackets are made in this type of fabric, rather like track-suit tops but with the rear pockets which are so useful. It isn't necessary to wear the ultra-close-fitting 'tights' that racing cyclists use, but stretchy leggings will generally be more comfortable than normal woven fabric slacks. If you prefer to wear slacks, there is nothing wrong in doing so, but it is important that you use cycle clips or, preferably, Velcro bands to prevent the bottoms of the trousers catching in the chain. Good cycling leggings will have a double seat, and some will have special inserts to make for more comfortable riding. Shorts, too, either the stretchy kind or the cooler polycotton, will have double seat and comfortable inserts. These inserts can also be bought separately from good cycle shops. Although many cyclists like to wear shorts in hot weather, remember that your knees and upper legs can burn easily, and it may be more comfortable to wear tracksuit-type trousers.

Outer garments

General purpose touring jackets for cyclists are quite popular and are widely advertised in the cycling press. They are made either from cotton fabric or from one of the breathable waterproof fabrics currently available. Most are lined and incorporate plenty of pockets, with adjustable tabs at the waistline, giving the garments a snug fit. The 'breathables' are particularly useful as they can be worn all the time when the weather is slightly 'doubtful', making it unnecessary to stop and put on additional rainwear when the rain does come down! Some people prefer to use a simple windshell jacket, which is lighter and less bulky than a touring jacket. Remember that your jacket needs to be long enough to protect the lumbar region. Generally speaking you will keep yourself warm when cycling, but when you stop you have to make sure that you do not chill. In very cold weather a lightweight insulated waistcoat could be useful to prevent chilling at such times.

Setting out for the day from a farm camp site. Note that the gear is packed into low-loader front panniers. (Derek Wood)

Rainwear

Traditionally, capes were always carried by cyclists for use in a downpour. These were made from heavy oiled fabric, and later PVC, but these days such garments are mostly made from lightweight proofed nylon, or from lightweight breathable fabrics. We cannot see the point of the latter, as capes have such a large air flow underneath that the pressure inside the garment can never be higher than that outside. Since breathable fabrics work only when the pressure inside is greater than that outside, the reduced efficiency of the breathable fabric will not justify the extra cost.

Capes do have the advantage that they are held over the handlebars of the cycle and therefore keep what is beneath it, including a large area of your legs, dry. However, their disadvantage is that your hand signals can be restricted, and in windy weather the cape can blow about rather a lot, and could be hazardous.

More and more cyclists are choosing to carry one of the relatively inexpensive cycling jackets made from a special stretchy PVC fabric with a bonded, knitted lining, which will keep off the worst of the rain. Despite being made of PVC, they are quite comfortable to wear and they do not seem to 'sweat' inside. Other useful jackets are made from lightweight Gore-Tex or other breathable fabrics and have integral hoods which are specially cut to move with the head. This is important for a cyclist, who needs to look behind, for example before turning right. Special lightweight proofed cycling suits are also available, with matching overtrousers that fit close to the ankles. Some have 'articulated knees' for extra freedom of movement. There are also some general purpose suits, designed for all activities such as running, jogging and cycling, which can be useful if you plan to walk and cycle but only want to buy one waterproof. These suits are light in weight and have the advantage that they often fold into their own pocket, making a 'bum bag' which can be worn around the waist, or attached to the handlebar or cross-bar of the cycle with short Velcro straps.

Some cyclists prefer to wear a light Pertex shell-suit. This will not keep off heavy rain, but the fabric is windproof and highly showerproof and dries very quickly in the wind. Despite the choice of waterproofs, many cyclists still contend that it is not worth stopping to don wet weather gear unless the rain is very heavy. They reckon that, with modern fabrics, water is not absorbed quickly, and when the rain stops the wind will soon dry your clothes. The choice is up to you, but we, for our part, prefer to use our waterproofs.

Visibility

Before we leave the subject of garments, make sure you are always clearly visible by wearing bright coloured clothing. An alternative is to wear a reflective bandolier or fluorescent mesh waistcoat, similar to that worn by road sweepers. Such things may be obtained from good cycle shops and chain stores.

Heads, Hands and Feet

Helmets

The question of protection for your head is important. There has been a lot of campaigning to try and get cyclists to wear a helmet, implying that if you wear one you will not be harmed if you have an accident. Unfortunately this is not as simple as it sounds, because wearing a helmet will not prevent serious bodily injury in the event of an accident. Be that as it may, a helmet could prevent you from suffering severe head injuries if you go over your handlebars and land on your head, provided that it fits you correctly and is properly fastened with a strap under the chin. It should not slip or move about on your head. Always choose a helmet which is stamped with a recognised safety standards approval, such as the BSI 'kitemark'. It is a good idea for children to wear helmets, because they could tumble off, but if you insist your child wears one, then perhaps you should wear one too! Never allow a child to cycle with the chinstrap undone.

We should also be concerned with protecting our heads from the weather. Since thirty per cent of your body heat will be lost from your head – and possibly more than this when cycling in cold weather, you will need to protect it. Most cyclists wear a simple woollen cap or bobble hat, although in winter time a balaclava may be more useful. In summer, a peaked cap is a good idea, as it shades the eyes and helps keep your vision clear. If it is very hot, remember to protect the back of your neck, which is very vulnerable on a bike. Some cotton caps are made with a protective flap sewn to the back edge, or you can sew a large handkerchief to an ordinary cap. Ladies may like to wear a cotton headscarf to stop their hair blowing into their eyes and at the same time protecting their neck. Some cyclists like to use the old-fashioned sou'wester to protect their heads in heavy rain. Another useful idea for wet weather is to wear a light neck-scarf, made from a piece of towelling, which will help prevent rain running down your neck.

Gloves and Socks

Track mitts protect your hands from pressure and are recommended. In hot weather, remember that the back of your hand under the central 'hole' may need some sun protection. In winter thermal gloves may be preferred, but ordinary thermal gloves do not give a good grip on the handlebars. Some special sticky thicky thermal gloves, made by Wild Country, are ideal for winter use on a bike, as they do provide a good grip. Cotton socks will be comfortable to wear in most conditions, and those with towelling or loop-stitched inners are ideal. Some of the new polyester loopstitch activity socks are most comfortable, dry quickly when wet and may be preferred. To prevent cold feet when cycling, try wearing wool socks instead of cotton ones. In very cold weather a pair of thin polypropylene or silk socks worn inside your normal socks may help. It is all a matter of personal choice.

Footwear

Footwear for cyclists should be comfortable. Always cycle in flat-heeled shoes, properly fastened with either Velcro or laces to support your feet. Personally speaking, we have always been happy to ride in trainers, and for those who only plan a little gentle riding these will be perfectly adequate. As you progress into cycling you may wish to buy proper cycling shoes. Whatever you choose to wear, bear in mind that at some stage you might have to get off your bike and push, so your shoes and socks need to fit well. Proper cycling shoes, with plates or cleats to retain their position on the pedals are favoured by what may be termed 'dedicated cyclists'. However, this type of shoe is most uncomfortable when you have to walk – and there will be such occasions – and a specialist shoe designed for the touring cyclist will be more practical. Looking rather like a lightweight leather training shoe, but with a definite, if very low, heel, it incorporates a special tread on the sole which gives a good grip on the pedals but is also suitable for walking. These shoes can be used with toe clips and/or straps if these are fitted to your bike. Their big advantage is that you can continue to wear them when sightseeing without hurting your feet. If you don't want to spend extra money on special shoes, then ordinary trainers are probably best. Whatever shoe you decide on it must fit properly, and have stiff soles to help pedalling. Lightly ridged soles prevent feet from slipping on the pedals.

Keeping out the wet

It is always difficult to keep your feet dry on a bike. Apart from rain itself, spray from the road and from passing traffic can soon soak your feet. Special cyclists' overshoes or spats, designed to fit over cycling shoes and made from waterproof neoprene are obtainable from good cycling shops. You could also wear a pair of Gore-Tex breathable socks over a pair of thin socks in place of your normal ones. As an alternative a pair of over-wellies (from a garden centre) will fit over trainers, or a simple pair of 'spats' could be home made from waterproof material, fitting under the toe of the shoe with a piece of neoprene rubber.

Not just clothes!

Cyclists will not only need suitable clothes and footwear on their persons. They will need to carry their food and a drink, as well as a spare jersey and waterproofs, and will require something in which to pack it all. It does not matter how short a distance you will be riding, the fact remains that to carry your needs in a carrier bag on the handlebars of your bike is not conducive to either comfort or safety!

Carrying your Kit

It is safest to carry your 'bits and pieces' actually on your cycle, rather than on your person. Obviously, a few Mars bars can go in your pocket, and some cyclists carry what they call a 'bonk bag' in which to carry a packed lunch. This is a small, square cotton bag with a web strap, which is worn over the shoulder. Better still, if you must wear something on your person, is a small 'bum bag', which will carry your waterproofs and maybe also your lunch. For a morning or afternoon ride, either of these bags would be O.K., but for a longer ride we suggest using a saddlebag or a bar bag. You will then be able to carry a camera safely, plus your lunch and snacks, waterproofs and some first aid kit. Not forgetting, of course, that you'll need to carry some bike tools. Drink bottles are usually carried in a special cage on the cycle, but they can also be carried in the side pocket of a saddle bag. We do know of mountain bikers who wear small rucksacks when riding, but we cannot recommend this as there is bound to be a certain amount of back movement as you ride, as well as sweating, and the two combined could make you feel very uncomfortable. Apart from this, any weight carried on your back can cause instability and result in an accident. Let the cycle carry the load, and keep the weight and centre of gravity as low as possible for a safer ride.

Out for the day with a trailer and a cycle seat.(Chris Juden)

Cycle bags should be made from hard-wearing waterproof materials, properly reinforced against abrasion, with good contoured flaps and well-shielded zips to prevent any ingress of rain. Saddlebags are available in a variety of sizes and materials, some of which have a dual flap to increase or decrease capacity as necessary. Bar bags, designed to fit the handlebars are useful to carry small items for a day's ride, and often have a transparent pocket on top for a map or guide book, which may be part of the flap or detachable. The top flap should open away from you, not only because you can get at the contents easily when sitting on the saddle, but also to keep out the rain. Make sure your bar bag has a proper support, so that it is held clear of the brake and gear cables, and do not carry too many heavy articles in it – use a saddle bag as well if need be. Families taking children on tandems may prefer to carry their kit in rear panniers, but these will not normally be needed for a day's ride. We will discuss these more fully in Chapter Nine.

Tools and adjustments

Even if going out for a morning or afternoon ride it is unwise to go without any tools, and your bike should be maintained in a safe condition. Always carry a pump, have a puncture repair kit with you and know how to use it, or carry a spare inner tube of the correct size for your cycle. Make sure you can use the tyre levers to remove the outer tyre from the wheel rim – if you can't do this, you won't be able to mend any puncture! Carry spanners to fit the various nuts on your cycle, in case any adjustment is needed, and make sure you can replace the chain if it comes off. An old rag and a small container of soft soap or 'Swarfega' can be useful to clean up your hands afterwards. On longer trips your tool kit should be more comprehensive, and include spare brake and gear cables, spokes and a spoke key, brake blocks, as well as tools to fit bottom bracket lockrings, pedals and wheel bearing cones. A pair of small pliers and screwdrivers to fit any screws on your machine will be useful, plus the appropriate sizes of Allen key for your particular cycle. A chain link remover and a spare inner tube should also be carried, plus a few spare nuts and bolts of suitable size for pannier carriers, as these can often work loose. The steering must be properly adjusted and lubricated, and the handlebars correctly positioned for your own comfort with no movement at the stem. Fix the saddle at the correct height so that when you sit on it both feet can just touch the ground. The chain should be adjusted to the correct tension and be properly oiled, and the wheels must be true with all spokes in position and undamaged. Check that the brakes are properly adjusted so you can stop easily and quickly; if necessary adjust and /or renew the brake blocks. Make sure the tyres are in good order, and pumped up hard to make pedalling easier. If there is any chance of your being out after dusk, ensure that the bike has good front and rear lights which conform to the legal requirements and are in working order. It goes without saying that you should always carry spare bulbs and batteries for your lamps.

Finally, it is worth obtaining a copy of the CTC Handbook, published by the Cyclists' Touring Club. This is free to members, but non-members may purchase a copy. It contains a mine of useful information for cyclists, including emergency repairers, taking cycles on trains, information on cycle crossings (bridges, tunnels and ferries) plus technical information. Also incorporated is an excellent accommodation guide arranged by county.

CHAPTER THREE

FINDING YOUR WAY

Map and compass – the very words seem to conjure up great mysteries in many peoples' minds, but basically, a map is only a sheet of paper and a compass is just a gadget which seems to work with a mind of its own. Maybe that's rather over-simplifying things, but knowing a little about using a map and a compass can add immensely to your enjoyment of your outings, even on the shortest walks or rides.

Why maps?

If you are following a route described in a Footpath Guide or in a magazine article, surely there will be some sort of map, even if only a simple diagram. True, but a good map covering the whole area can add so much to the pleasure of the trip. Maps are fascinating records which not only show what you will see on the ground but give clues about the history of the landscape, and what you might find on the other side of the hill or wood. Maps will help you to extend your travels away from the signed route you are following, and enable you to plan your own wanderings into more interesting parts. Even before you go, an evening at home just browsing over a good map can be a surprisingly enjoyable experience, and the same can be said of re-living your wanderings on your return.

What is a map?

A map is a simplified diagram on a flat sheet of paper of what we would expect to see on the ground. A photograph taken from the air, looking straight down, may be unclear due to variations in the light or the time of day or season of the year. The map-maker tries to overcome these problems by using a system of simple *Conventional Signs* and symbols. Another big problem is how to represent the ground, which is often far from flat, on a flat sheet of paper. The map needs to show the *position*, *shape* and *size* of objects on the ground, their *distance* apart, and the *shape* of the ground itself, together with the type of vegetation, woods, fields, lakes and streams. In short, a map should show the *physical features*, both natural and man-made, which we can actually see on the ground. A good map will show all this, together with other information which cannot be seen but is just as important to us as walkers or cyclists. Examples of this include details of Rights of Way, public access land, National Trust property, MOD Danger Areas, and sites of historic interest. The list of useful information seems endless, and the map-maker's dilemma must always be to decide how much to include and how much to leave out.

What kind of map?

There are many different types of map intended for different purposes. Simple sketch maps with very little surrounding detail may be used to illustrate written route descriptions. Motorists travelling long distances require maps covering a large area of country with clear indication of classified roads, and information relating to service stations and emergency telephones, but very little detailed information about the intervening countryside. The walker and cyclist may not be concerned so much with major roads, but much more detail about the actual countryside, footpaths, bridleways and so on, is vital. Some idea of the 'ups and downs' of the ground is also of great significance – in fact, what is needed is sufficient information to enable the map reader to form a mental picture of the scene beforehand. To achieve this is the ultimate aim of the map-maker's art and the map-reader's skill.

Map scales

The map cannot, of course, be the same size as the area of land it portrays. It must be reduced and a measure of this reduction in size is given by the *scale* of the map. A very popular scale used in this country up until a few years ago was the 'One Inch' scale, or more precisely, "one inch to one statute mile". This simply means that a distance of one inch on the map represents one mile on the ground. Maps to this scale are still to be found. However, with the introduction of Metrication, the nearest equivalent today is a scale of two centimetres on the map to one kilometre on the ground, approximately equal to 1¼ inches on the map to one mile on the ground. This is a very clumsy way of describing scale, so what is known as a *representative fraction* or *ratio* is used. For example, 1:50,000 simply means that a distance of one unit on the map equals 50,000 units on the ground – one centimetre on the map represents 50,000 centimetres (one half kilometre) on the ground.

Two very useful map scales for use by walkers and cyclists are 1:25,000 and 1:50,000. These are approximately 2½ inches to one mile (1:25,000) and, as we have already seen, 1¼ inches to one mile (1:50,000). The former is a *larger* scale than the latter; a good way to remember the difference is to realise that on a given size of paper, a large scale map covers less ground with more detail.

A selection of Ordnance Survey maps for walkers and cyclists

Map types

Ordnance Survey maps provide complete coverage of England, Wales and Scotland and set the standard by which others are judged. For walkers and cyclists, the Ordnance Survey produces several series of maps to different scales, all based on accurate survey data with the addition of useful information relating to tourist attractions, Rights of Way, historical sites and other subjects.

1:50,000 scale: 'Landranger' series covers the whole country on 204 sheets, and is suitable for cycling or general walking in country where great detail is not necessary to be shown on the map.

1:25,000 scale: 'Pathfinder' series of maps cover most of the country in much more detail, including field boundaries, making them particularly useful for walkers in lowland areas where farmland is predominant. The disadvantage is that the sheet size is small, covering an area 1km by 2km, so a number of separate sheets may be required for one journey. The most popular walking areas of the country are covered by 'Outdoor Leisure' maps, to the same scale and with additional detail of use to walkers. They cover a much larger area than the standard Pathfinder sheets, their main disadvantage being that the sheet size makes them difficult to handle in windy conditions. A more recent addition to the range, again at this scale, is the 'Explorer' series, the first sheets of which were published early in 1994. These fill a gap between the Pathfinder and Outdoor Leisure series, covering other attractive areas and although not as large as the Outdoor Leisure sheets, they depict an area larger than 2km by 1 km. The whole country will be covered at a scale of 1:25,000 by one or other of the above three series of maps.

A complete index to the 1:50,000 and 1:25,000 OS maps is available free on request from major map retailers, or in case of difficulty direct from OS head office (address in Chapter Ten)

1:250,000 scale: For touring cyclists who plan long rides going well beyond the boundaries of the Landranger map sheets, the new 'Travelmaster' maps, although intended mainly for motorists, can prove very useful. The scale is approximately one inch to four miles.

Harveys maps cover popular walking and climbing areas

Harveys Maps, produced by Harveys, of Doune in Perthshire, cover many of the most popular walking and climbing areas in England, Scotland and Wales. Their 'Walker's Map' series at a scale of 1:40,000 and, more recently, their 'Superwalker' series at a scale of 1:25,000 are specially designed for use by hill walkers and climbers. Both make use of the National Grid and are printed on tough waterproof paper. Contours at 15m intervals are very clearly shown to emphasise the dips and slopes of the ground, and colour overlays depict differences in surface vegetation. The same firm has introduced a series of 'Touring Maps' at 1:100,000 scale, also on waterproof paper, aimed particularly at cyclists.

Much of the information we are discussing applies to maps in general, but specific details will refer mainly to maps in the Ordnance Survey series.

Signs and Symbols

Maps use simple signs and symbols to represent various objects and features. As far as possible, they are clear and self-explanatory, but there will always be a key or legend printed somewhere on the sheet which lists all those used. With practice, the map user will become familiar with the most common symbols, although it is as well to check as they can vary from edition to edition and from scale to scale. Roads, tracks and paths are distinguished, and so are railways – good features to confirm your position even if you do not intend to catch a train! The same applies to rivers, streams and canals. Woods, heath, sand dunes, beaches and mud flats all have their distinctive appearance on the various map types. When it comes to man-made features, prominent structures such as churches, radio or TV masts, windmills and towers are all good aids to navigation, and as such are shown clearly on the maps. Administrative boundaries are perhaps not so important to the walker or cyclist, but these are shown – so make sure you know the difference between their symbols and those used for footpaths and tracks. With the limitations imposed on the map maker by space and the restrictions of the colour printing process used, it is amazing how much information there is on one sheet of paper.

Distance and direction

In addition to the list of signs and symbols, every map sheet will state the scale, as a representative fraction (e.g. 1:25,000) and will have a small scale showing major units (kilometres or miles) and sub-units, in both metric and Imperial units. This enables you to measure distances on the map. All maps, including sketch maps illustrating route descriptions, should have an indication of scale.

It is normal practice for map sheets to be printed with the top edge towards the north and the sides running north-south. Somewhere on the map, usually in one margin, there will be a diagram and information relating to three different north directions! We will discuss this in more detail when describing the use of a compass, but for most purposes we only need to remember that north is at the top of the map.

Position finding on the map

Navigators at sea often use latitude and longitude to describe their position, but for a number of reasons this is not very convenient for use on land when dealing with relatively small distances, so the National Grid was devised during the 1940s. This covers the whole country with an imaginary network of squares with sides 100km long. Each square is sub-divided into squares of 1km and the lines forming these smaller squares are printed on all the 1:50,000 and 1:25,000 map sheets. Each of the vertical and horizontal lines forming these squares is numbered in the margins with two figures running in sequence from west (left) to east (right) and from south (bottom) to north (top). The numbers in each case lie between 00 and 99, after which they are repeated. The vertical line numbers increase from west to east, so these lines are called *eastings*; the horizontal lines are numbered from south to north, so are called *northings*. Whatever the scale, these lines are always spaced the equivalent of one kilometre on the ground. Landranger maps have these lines and numbers printed in blue, with every tenth line made bolder; on the latest editions the numbers are repeated across the face of the map. The grid lines and numbers are black on the 1:25,000 series.

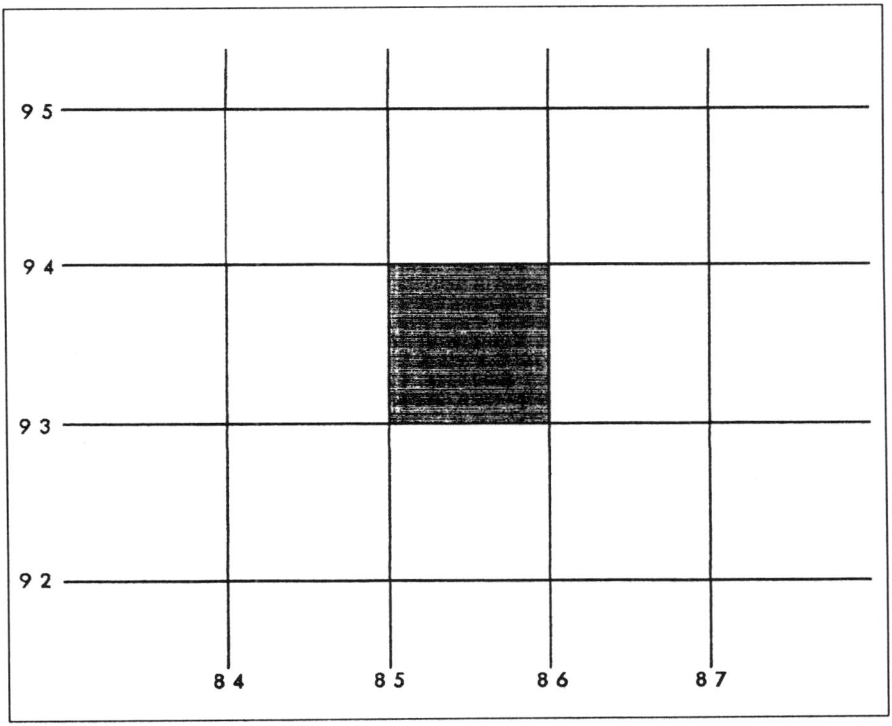

Fig 3.1. Reference of 1km square square is 8593

Any 1km square on the map can be described by the numbers of the grid lines bounding it. First, locate the nearest *easting* line to the left of the square and note its two-digit number, then the two-digit number of the *northing* line below the square is noted. In diagram 3.1 showing a section of a grid the shaded square has a Grid Reference (GR) of 8593. To find the GR of a smaller point on the map, for example a church, imagine each side of the 1km square to be sub-divided into tenths, as shown in diagram 3.2. Then estimate how many tenths of the square lie between the left side and the point, making the third digit in the *easting*. Finally, estimate the number of tenths up from the bottom of the square to give the final digit of the *northing*. The complete 6-figure Grid Reference comprises three digits for the easting followed by three digits for the northing, giving 856937 for the example in our diagram. This defines a point within 100m on the ground. A number of simple ways can be used to remember the sequence—'along the passage and up the stairs' is one—meaning that you read the *easting* before the *northing*.

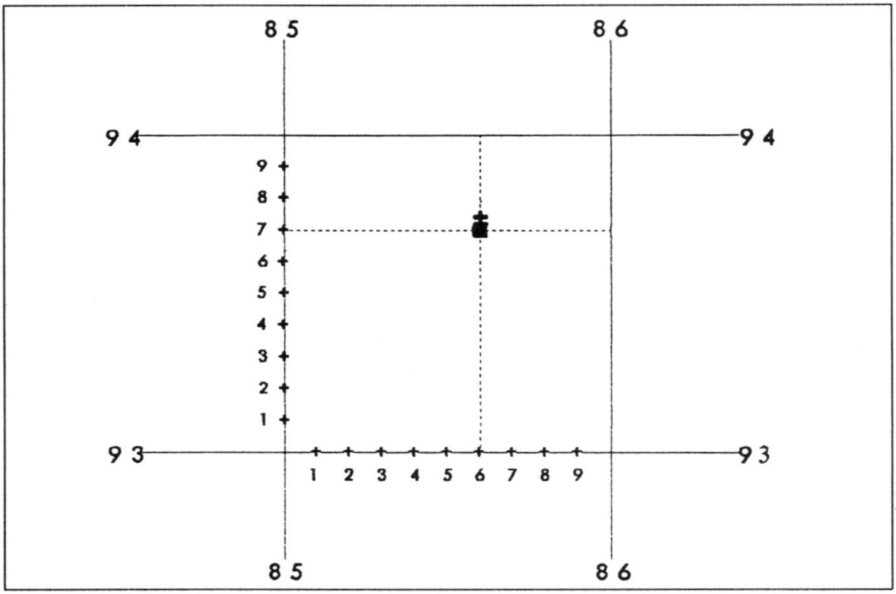

Fig 3.2. Grid Reference of church is 856937

Since the numbering of the lines runs from 00 to 99 then repeats, it follows that a reference of six digits will be repeated every 100km in an easterly and northerly direction. This will not matter if we are working on only one or two adjacent map sheets. A simple way to avoid confusion is to give the sheet

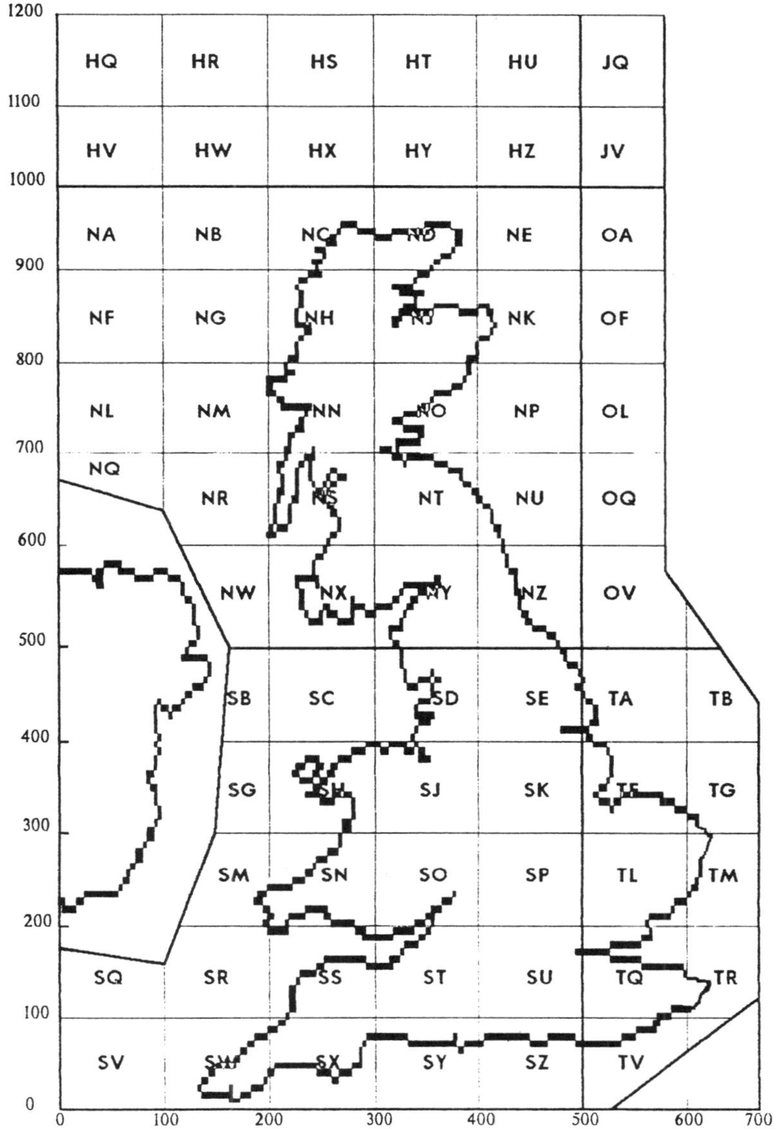

Fig 3.3. The National Grid – approximate locations of 100km squares

number of the map, followed by the GR. For example, 197/856937 tells us that the church is shown on sheet 197 of the Landranger map. However, when using small scale maps such as the Travelmaster series, the National Grid system can provide a unique reference for any position. The eastings and northings forming the 100km squares as mentioned at the beginning of this section are numbered 100, 200, and so on, and each square is designated by a pair of letters as shown in diagram 3.3. Every O.S. map sheet, regardless of its scale, carries a diagram showing which 100km square or squares are covered by it. To return to our example, the complete and unique GR for our church can be given as SZ 856937, and this Grid Reference can only apply to one point in the whole country.

Note that if a point lies exactly on an easting or northing line, the third or sixth figures must be quoted as 0, so maintaining a total of six digits. To locate a point on the map for which you know the reference, the above procedure is reversed. First, locate the line bearing the first two numbers, and estimate the tenths, working from left to right, then do the same working up the map from the bottom. This should bring you to the point required. Obviously, it helps to know what the point is, such as a cross-roads, a church, or other marked feature, since the reference can only be to the nearest 100m and there may well be a church near the cross-roads.

With practice it becomes easy to estimate the tenths, but for more accurate measurement a simple device called a *romer* can be used. This is a small scale on plastic or card, marked to indicate tenths of a 1km grid square, according to the scale of map in use. The markings run along two sides, at right angles, and the corner of the romer is placed on the point on the map whose reference is required, as shown in diagram 3.4. Where the *easting* and *northing* lines cut the scale, the third and sixth figures of the reference can be read off. Romers are available calibrated

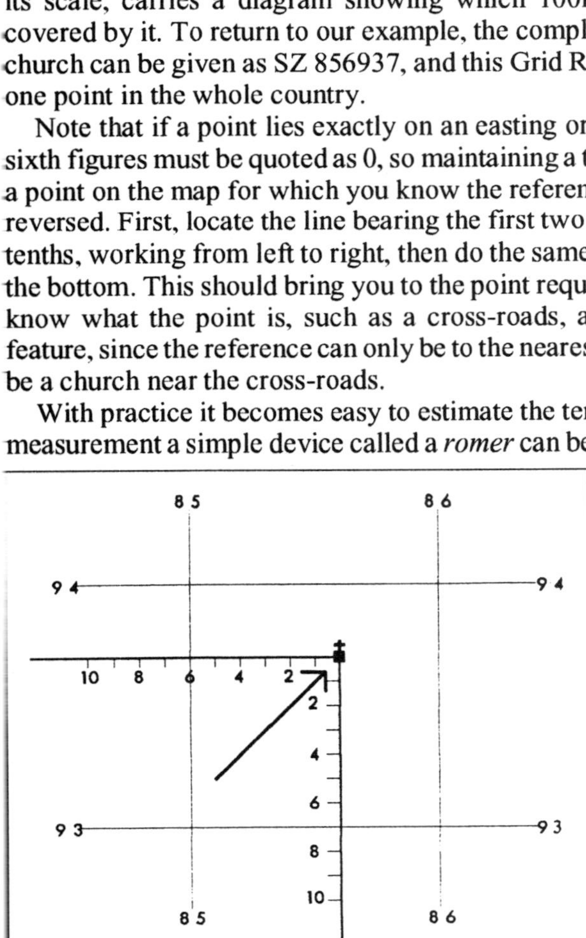

Fig 3.4. Romer measures Grid Reference of church to be 856937

for different map scales, and some compasses have romer scales on their base plates.

The shape of the landscape

The map is flat, but the countryside is far from flat, and how to present a true picture of the lie of the land has been a problem since maps were invented.

The height or altitude of any point on the ground in this country is referred to *mean sea level*, which is determined at Newlyn in Cornwall. On the map, a number printed beside a dot shows the height in metres above this reference datum. This is known as a *spot height*, and will often be found along roads, or at the tops of hills. Although an accurate measure of altitude at a point, the use of spot heights gives little idea of the direction or steepness of slopes, information which is very important to walkers and cyclists.

The usual way of describing the ups and downs makes use of *contour lines*, which are lines on the map joining points which have the same height above sea level. On the Landranger maps the lines are orange in colour, drawn at *vertical intervals* of 10 metres, while the 1:25,000 maps of the Pathfinder, Outdoor Leisure and Explorer series have the contours at intervals of either 10 or 5 metres, depending on the type of ground – lowland areas will have a 5 metre interval while upland areas with steeper slopes are covered by contours at 10 metre spacing. Every fifth line is drawn slightly thicker, and the height is marked in breaks in the lines. Rising or falling ground is shown by these numbers and by the fact that they are printed with the tops of the figures towards the higher side. By studying the run of the contours, and noting spot heights and realising that streams and rivers run through dips and valleys, a mental picture of the terrain can be built up. A closed loop in a contour will usually mean that the ground within the loop is at the top of rising ground, and closely-spaced contours occur where there are steep slopes. Diagram 3.5 shows a simple contour plot, together with a profile or section of the ground it represents. Where the contour spacing gets closer towards higher ground the slope will be concave, and when the closer spacing is followed by gradually increased spacing the indication is that the steep slope is levelling off near the top, in a convex profile.

Other ways of representing height and relief are used, such as *layer-colouring*, *hill shading*, and a technique popular in earlier times known as *hachuring*. The first two methods may be found in conjunction with contours and spot heights and some of the current Tourist Maps are real works of art, presenting a three-dimensional effect.

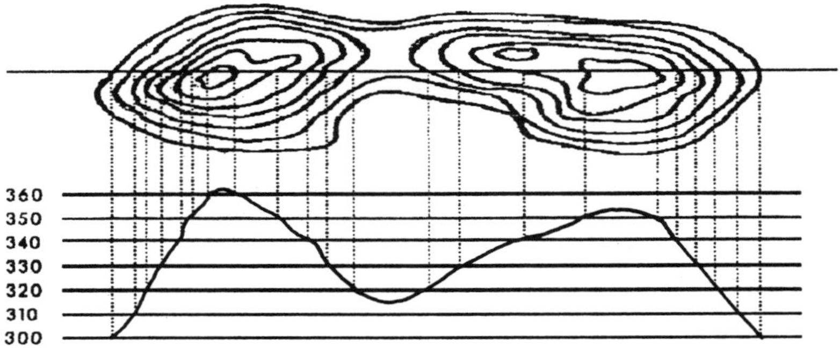

Fig 3.5. A contour plot with a vertical section

A sense of direction

It is much easier to identify features on the ground and to decide which is the right way to go if your map is *set* or *oriented* so that objects you can see from your present position and their symbols on the map lie in the same relative directions. The simplest way to set the map if you are standing on a straight road or track is to turn the map until the feature aligns with what is on the ground, making sure you haven't got it completely upside down! Check this by noting other adjacent features and their relative positions. Another way is to pick out some prominent landmarks, two or preferably three, then hold the map level and turn it so that the landmarks are in line with their positions as shown on the map. When following a route, keep the map set in this way so that turns in the route and interesting features can be identified and there will be less risk of missing a turning. For many walks and rides this will be quite sufficient. At the beginning of this chapter we noted that maps are printed with their top edge towards the north, so when setting the map by observing objects on the ground we have also found the approximate direction of north.

Which north?

This is not a 'consumer's best buy' guide – in fact, there are three different north directions to consider. First is *True North*, the direction towards the geographical North Pole, which is really only of interest to the map makers. As map users we are more interested in the other north directions. One of these is *Magnetic North*(MN), the direction in which the magnetised needle of a compass points. The Magnetic North Pole is in northern Canada at present, but it has the habit of slowly changing its position over many years and varies in different parts of the country, a fact which will not bother us overmuch unless we want to get involved in very accurate navigation over long distances. Finally there is *Grid North* (GN), which is the direction in which the vertical lines of the National Grid, (and the left and right edges of O.S. maps) point. Grid North is a fixed direction based on the parallel lines of the National Grid.

Bearings

A *bearing* is a direction, measured in degrees, in relation to North, and is always measured in a clockwise direction. For example, East = 90°, South = 180°, West = 270° and North = 0° or 360°. We are concerned with either Magnetic bearings, measured with a compass relative to Magnetic North, or Grid bearings relative to Grid North. The difference between them is equal to the *Magnetic Variation* (MV). On all OS map sheets the MV is given for a given date together with a note of the annual change, often accompanied by a small diagram similar to Diagram 3.6. At present it is around 5° West in the centre of the country, that is to say MN is 5° west of GN.

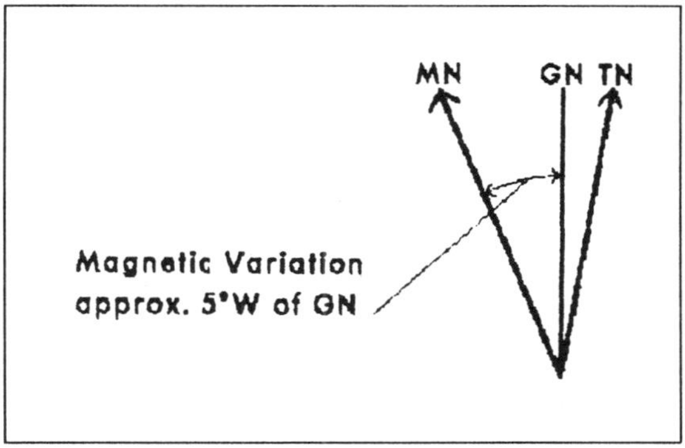

Fig 3.6. The 3 North Points

The compass

In theory a compass can just be a magnetised needle hanging from a thread, but this is not very practical for use in the field! A typical compass for walkers has the needle pivoted in a sealed capsule or housing filled with liquid to smooth its movement. The capsule is mounted on a transparent baseplate and can be rotated. The baseplate carries various markings which can be seen in the next photograph, which shows a SILVA Type 3 compass. Other models and makes may have different features, but the minimum requirement should be a rotating capsule with degree markings, orienting lines and a direction-of-travel arrow.

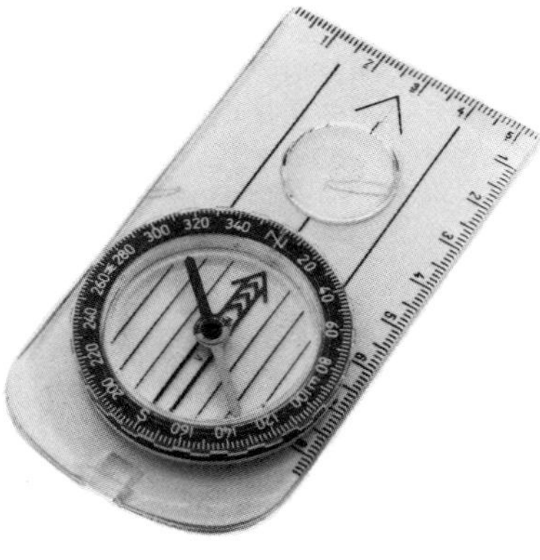

SILVA Compass Type 3; diagram below shows major features:

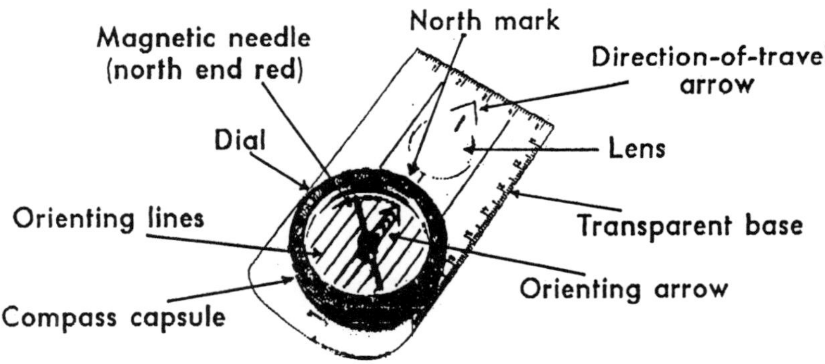

SILVA Type 3 Compass

More sophisticated models may have sighting arrangements whereby the distant object and its bearing on the compass can be read simultaneously. The simplest versions have a folding mirror with a sighting slit or notch. When looking towards a distant object the position of the compass needle can be seen in the mirror together with the degree markings. An example is the SILVA Type 27 shown in the picture below. Luminous spots on the needle and sighting points enable the instrument to be used at night. Cheap compasses

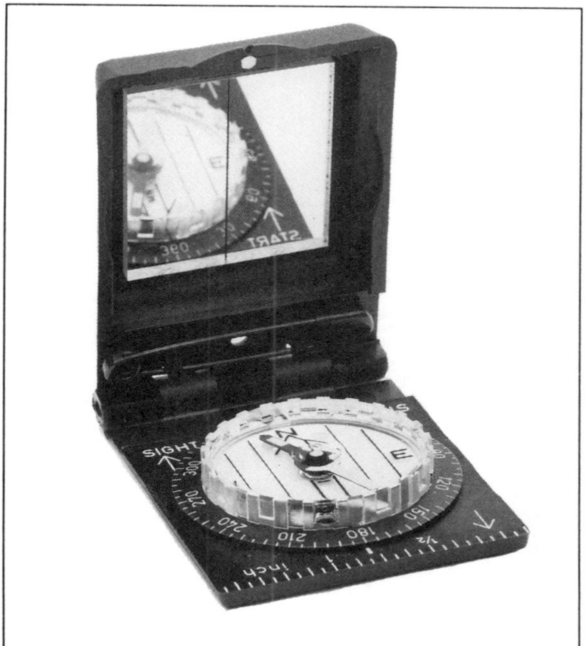

SILVA Compass Type 27 has a sighting mirror.

with just a simple needle and no sealed liquid-filled capsule are hardly worth buying, as their accuracy and reliability will be suspect.

Take care of your compass

Your compass is a precision instrument. Keep it away from strong magnets, electrical machines or loudspeakers, and keep it clean. For carrying, a small wallet or pouch is useful, but when out walking, attach a cord lanyard to the baseplate so the compass can hang around your neck; alternatively, pass the cord around a shirt or jacket button and carry the compass in your pocket, so that if you drop it you won't lose it. Good quality compasses are quite rugged but at very low temperatures or very high altitudes small bubbles may form within the capsule. These will disappear on return to more normal conditions. Occasionally, check the needle for free movement and, when using the compass, do not hold it near any ferrous metal objects. These include wire fences, gates, knives, cameras, metal belt buckles or your bicycle frame!

Setting the map with a compass

Turn the compass capsule on its baseplate until the North mark is opposite the Direction-of-Travel line, then lay the compass on the map and line up one edge of the baseplate along one of the north-south Grid lines on the map. Holding them together, turn the map until the North (red) end of the needle points to N on the rim of the capsule, and the map will then be *roughly* set to align with the terrain.

Check your position on the ground with your map.

For a more exact setting, allow for Magnetic Variation. Assuming this is 5° West, turn the map and compass until the needle points to 355° and not to N. This avoids having to remember any calculations and will be sufficiently accurate for most parts of Great Britain.

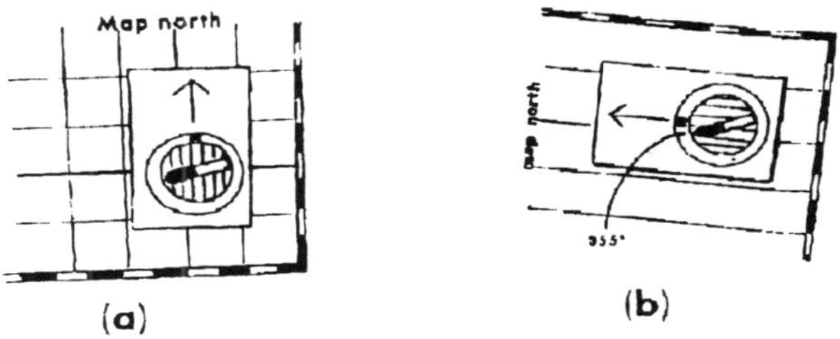

Fig 3.7. Setting the map with a compass.

Walking in the right direction

If you want to reach a distant point such as a prominent landmark and you can walk over open moorland, hold your compass level and point the Direction-of-Travel arrow towards your destination. Then turn the capsule until the N on the rim is opposite the red end of the needle. Look in the direction of the arrow and note some object, such as a tree or bush, which lies on your course. Walk until you reach that point, then holding the compass level and without moving the capsule, turn the whole instrument until the needle again lines up with the N mark. Take another look ahead in the direction of travel and note another landmark. Continue in this way until you reach your final destination. Check your course at intervals. If trees or dips and bumps in the ground make you lose sight of your destination, by aiming at intermediate points which lie on your line then rechecking with the compass, you can still reach your objective, even if you have to make a diversion in between. Do not walk along with your head down, looking at the compass – choose a target well ahead and go for it! This way, you have no need to worry about bearings or magnetic variation.

Fig 3.8. Setting a compass course to a distant point

What is the right direction?

When you cannot see your destination, or perhaps you want to check which path is the right one to take, lay the edge of the compass on the map along the path you want or between your start and finish points, making sure the Direction-of-Travel arrow points from your start point towards the finishing point. Holding the compass still on the map, turn the capsule until the N mark is towards the top (North) of the map.

Fig 3.9. Finding a bearing from the map

Parallel orienting lines on the bottom of the capsule help this by being lined up with the vertical Grid lines on the map. This has set the Grid Bearing on your compass, which has been used as a protractor. The map can be put away, and holding the compass level and turning it until the red end of the needle aligns with the N mark on the rim of the capsule, the Direction-of-Travel arrow points in the direction you want. Note that you have made no allowance for Magnetic Variation. Usually in good visibility this will not matter, as you would only be about 9 metres off course in a distance of 100 metres, slightly to the left. To correct for this error simply turn the compass until the needle lines up with the 355° mark instead of the N mark. No calculations needed!

What is that feature?

To identify a distant feature such as a prominent hilltop or one of several church towers, point the Direction-of-Travel arrow towards the feature and, holding the compass level, turn the capsule until the red end of the needle aligns with the N mark on the rim (or with the 355° mark). Lay the compass on your map with one long edge just touching your own position on the map. Hold the map still and turn the whole compass around until N on the capsule rim points towards the top of the map and the orienting lines lie parallel to the north-south Grid Lines on the map. Then the distant object will be somewhere along the edge of the compass or on a line extending from it (Fig 3.10).

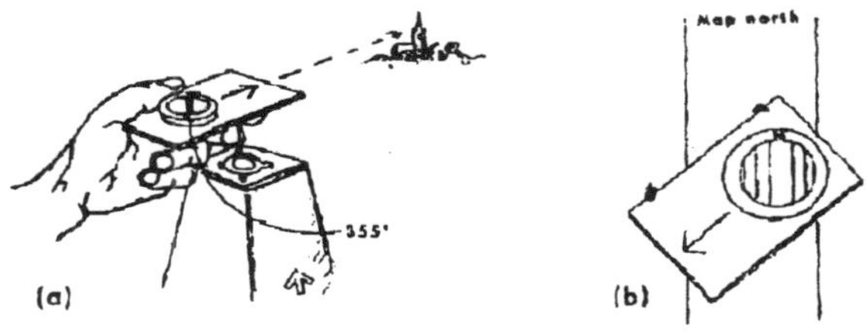

Fig 3.10. Identifying a feature using the compass

Where are you?

Maybe you want to know how far you are along a road, a stream or a ridge. Look for a distant feature at about right angles to your path which you can identify on the map. Point the compass towards it and turn the capsule until the needle points to N (or 355°) on the rim. Lay the compass on the map with its edge touching the distant feature and turn the whole compass until the red orienting lines are parallel to the north-south Grid Lines with the N mark towards the top of the map. Your position on the road will be where the edge of the compass base cuts it. If your own position is not too easily pin-pointed on the map you will need to sight on two, or preferably three distant objects, and draw pencil lines along the edge of the compass from each feature. Where these cut will be your position, and with a little care quite a satisfactory plot of your position can be made in this way (Fig 3.11).

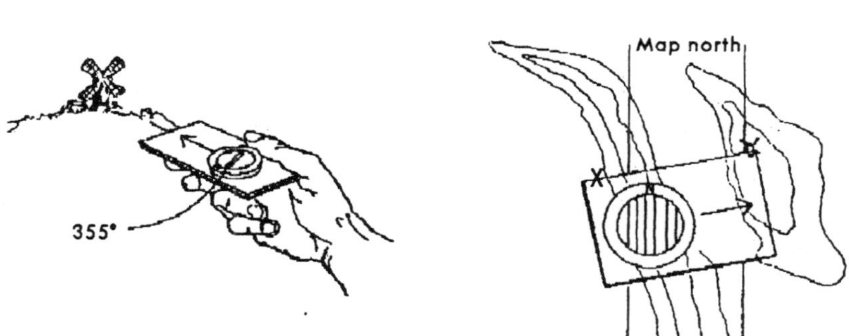

Fig 3.11. Finding position on the map

Back Bearings

When following a compass course across country it makes sense to check behind you occasionally, to see if you are still on course. Alternatively, you may want to return the way you came, following the same bearing in the reverse direction – on the *back bearing*. The simple way to do this is to retain the original setting on your compass and turn around until the *white* or South end of the compass needle points to the N mark (or 355° mark for better accuracy). Then follow the Direction-of-Travel arrow as before. This avoids any need to remember whether to add or subtract 180° from the original bearing (Fig 3.12).

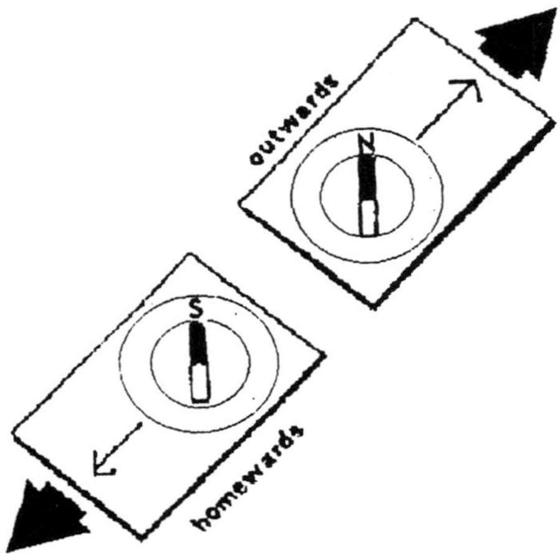

Fig 3.12. A simple way of using Back Bearings

Putting theory into practice

Try out the methods just described, and you will see they are not very complicated. Practice in different types of landscape, using different scales of map – the methods are still the same. The more you use your map the more familiar you will become with the various signs and symbols. Don't worry about trying to learn them all off by heart in the beginning, because every map sheet has a key to the signs printed inside the cover, in the margin or in a box down one side. In the same way, practice will enable you to read the map in the same way as you read a book, and to visualise what the landscape looks like before you see it in reality. This will help you planning your route if you are not following one already described in a guidebook, or one which is signposted for you.

Always keep a check on your map, noting as you go along the different features such as fields or wooded areas, boundary fences, buildings, overhead power lines, and so on. Keep your finger moving on the map as you go, so you can check your position. There will be times when, even if you are following a signed footpath, you come across a junction in tracks which seems confusing. Little used tracks become overgrown, or forestry or other work will form temporary tracks which are not shown on the map. This is where a quick look at your compass can confirm the right way to go.

If you are crossing a stretch of open country such as moorland, with no well defined track, there may be many animal tracks which lead anywhere except where you want to go – this is where your compass can prove invaluable, using the methods described above. Then comes the time when perhaps a sudden mist comes down or low cloud blots out the distant view. If this should happen, try to get a compass bearing on your destination point before it disappears from view. Check this with a bearing from your map, set it on your compass, then continue to follow it as described under the section "Walking in the right direction". Even in poor visibility it should be possible to line up your compass on a point a little distance ahead. Alternatively, send a companion to walk ahead as far as you can see, move to right or left until on the line you want to follow, then you join him or her – and continue in this way, leap-frogging until you reach the end. The main problem will be trying to reach a particular point, such as a stile in a fence or the corner of a wall which is not visible from your present position, and which may not be visible from a short distance away. The difficulty can be understood when you realise that the combined error in an average compass, together with your own error in setting and reading it, can easily be 4° either way. This means that in a distance of 1km you can miss your target by as much as 150m, enough to lose sight of it completely in difficult conditions. In such a situation the safest way is to "aim off", that is to set your course to a point to right or left of your target on some feature, identified on the map, such as a stream or fence, or the edge of a wood. When you reach this feature you simply turn and follow it to your destination.

The feature you aim for is known as a *line feature*, and a little care is needed in deciding whether to aim to the right or to the left of your target, depending on the terrain. Even when your target is a point, such as an isolated tree or stone cross on the moor, there is often some line feature near enough to act as a sort of "long stop", from which you can re-set your course to your destination.

When navigating in this way it is very useful to be able to estimate distances reasonably accurately, and one way is by counting your paces. First, you need to establish the average length of your *normal* pace. To do this, measure out, say, 100m and pace it several times in each direction, then calculate the average. It is vitally important that you take a normal, relaxed pace, and don't try to make it artificially even. Also, try it out on varying ground. A simple "clicker" counter is used by some people to keep the score, but you may devise your own way of counting.

Another way of checking distance covered is by time. Walking as before over a known distance, note the time taken. Check this several times and find your own average walking speed. Don't forget to allow time for stopping to check bearings and so on, but timing over a longer distance can be more useful than counting paces. We will have another look at this question of time in the next chapter.

A few final tips

If you want to draw lines or make notes on your map use a soft pencil which will rub out easily when you have finished, and keep your map clean and dry in a transparent map case. A few maps are available printed on waterproof paper, or you may try treating them with a waterproof solution such as Grangers' 'MapDry' or water-based 'Map Proof' from Nikwax.

Triangulation pillars, or 'Trig Points' as they are commonly called, are white-painted concrete pillars, often in prominent places, and shown on the maps as a small blue triangle with a dot inside on the Landranger maps or black on 1:25,000 maps of the OS. These make very good aiming marks and can provide welcome confirmation of your position, but since modern technology is making a number of these redundant they may not be as well maintained in future. Plans exist whereby organisations can adopt unwanted pillars with a view to maintaining them in good condition, but this may not apply to all of them. However, it is unlikely they will all disappear for many years to come and it is understood they will still be shown on the maps. Do not expect absolute accuracy when taking bearings – the combined error of your compass and your ability to read the scales may be quite sufficient for most situations, but if you want to allow for Magnetic Variation try sticking a small piece of adhesive tape under the compass capsule below the rim and mark where the 355° calibration should be – then use that mark instead of the N mark on the scale for aligning the needle. That will be good enough for most places in Great Britain. Above all, don't forget to keep clear of metal fences and other objects when using the compass – and trust your compass even if you think it is leading you astray!

CHAPTER FOUR

WHERE CAN YOU GO?

When planning a walk or ride the choice is almost limitless. How experienced are you – or how fit? Who is going with you? Is it a family group with young children? How much time have you? All these and many more questions come to mind, but the overriding factor should be your enjoyment of the experience.

Why?

Well, the exercise is good for you, but maybe that's not the best reason for going out! Perhaps there are some wonderful views, or attractive scenery. Maybe there are interesting old buildings on the route, country parks, picturesque villages, nature reserves or other reasons associated with your own special interests or hobbies. Some people enjoy walking or cycling as activities in their own right, or perhaps as a challenge, but for others they are just a means to an end which will play a major part in deciding the route to follow.

There are many ready-made routes such as those described in books published by Sigma Leisure, or other books and magazines. Many local authorities have established walks or cycle routes, often waymarked and described in leaflets or booklets published locally. The National Trails and many long distance walking routes have been the subject of numerous guidebooks. In case you think these would be too much to attempt, they can often be split into sections and often there are circular walks based on the main trails. Whether or not you decide to make use of published, waymarked routes or to choose your own route after studying maps, a certain amount of planning will help towards your enjoyment and safe return.

Where can you go?

Public roads are maintained by the local highway authority and may be used by anyone, from walkers to lorries – except that motorways are understandably banned to walkers and cyclists. On OS maps public roads are coloured and apart from minor country roads and lanes they are not of great interest to walkers. However, many quiet country lanes without too much traffic can provide excellent routes for cycling. In addition, OS maps depict uncoloured or white roads which are often unsurfaced and may be driveways leading to farms or houses, farm tracks or old green lanes or drove roads. It doesn't follow that because such routes are shown on the map the public can use them all.

Crossing the river by stepping stones in Dovedale

Rights of Way

Quite apart from the quiet country roads and lanes, our country is covered by a network of footpaths, bridleways and tracks, totalling more than 200,000km. These are shown on OS and other maps, but a few words about their use by the general public may settle a number of queries. All local authorities in England and Wales are required to establish the existence of routes over which the public has a right to pass, with certain limitations. These rights of way are recorded on a 'definitive map' maintained by the authority, and which may be inspected by members of the public. This establishes the legal right of passage along the route, even if it crosses private land, and there are several different types of right of way.

Footpaths are for use by walkers only, but where practicable, prams, push-chairs or wheelchairs may be taken on them.

Bridleways may be followed on foot, on horseback, or on a pedal-cycle, but motor cyclists have no legal right to use such a way.

Roads used as public paths (RUPPs) have the same rights of public use as a bridleway. A RUPP may, for example, be a private farm road over which the right of way has been established and duly recorded. The owner or tenant may, of course, drive vehicles on it.

Waymarked walks sometimes follow minor roads

Byways open to all traffic are a fourth category of right of way, where motor vehicles may be encountered although the primary use is likely to be as for a bridleway..

The definitive map information is supplied to the Ordnance Survey to enable it to be recorded on their various maps. Unfortunately, all local authorities are not equally up-to-date in supplying this information, so some indication of the date of the information is given on map sheets. On OS Landranger maps the different categories of right of way are shown in red, using different symbols. Owing to the small scale, care needs to be taken when using them to avoid confusion with other symbols such as administrative boundaries. Similar symbols, in green, are used on OS 1:25,000 maps, and at the larger scale they are easier to distinguish. Well-used paths and tracks will be clear to see on the ground, but often lack of use or, it has to be said, neglect on the part of landowners, makes it difficult to follow overgrown paths even when they are shown on the map. This is where a compass can be useful. There may also be paths which, although their existence is apparent on the ground, do not carry legal right of way status. These may be shown in black on the map. Some may be **permissive paths** along which the owner permits the public to go but has not agreed the right to go.

Rights of way should be signed, at least where they leave a road. Permissive paths are often signed, and many routes are waymarked. A scheme commonly followed is for footpaths to be signed with small yellow arrows and bridleways with blue arrows. **National Trails** often have an acorn sign associated with the arrows, and other long distance paths may have appropriate logos on their waymarks.

Walkers are allowed on most **canal towpaths**, some of which are rights of way. Cyclists are allowed to use towpaths of canals under the control of the British Waterways Board, subject to certain restrictions; permits are required but they are issued free on request.

Access to open country

All land is owned by someone. The public has right of access to public open spaces such as country parks, official picnic sites and similar places. Public access to some areas of open country such as heath, moorland, and some large estates has been granted by the owners; information has only recently been made available to enable this to be shown on some Outdoor Leisure maps, and there may be certain restrictions during, for example, grouse shooting periods. Notices at access points will explain the situation. Other places, particularly high moorland, are open by long-established custom, and the public is allowed entry to many areas of National Trust and Forestry Commission land, subject to conditions laid down by those bodies.

There is no doubt about this Permissive Path on the edge of the Lincolnshire fens

Walking in Scotland

The legal position regarding rights of way in Scotland differs from that in England and Wales. There is no obligation on local authorities to record rights of way on definitive maps. However, in general the public has access to most paths and tracks, and to open country, provided no hindrance is caused to the legitimate interests of farmers, sportsmen and foresters. Landowners may close areas at certain times of the year in connection with, for example, deer stalking or grouse shooting.

Rights and privileges

The final word on this question of access to paths or open country must be that everyone, both walker, cyclist or landowner/tenant, has some rights and some responsibilities. You are intending to enjoy your leisure activity, whereas people who live and work in the countryside must have a somewhat different outlook. Nevertheless, with some mutual understanding there need be no conflict of interest. The town dweller must realise that grass in a field is as much a crop as a field of wheat or cabbages, and it must not be trodden down or damaged by lighting fires. Gates left open can allow animals worth many hundreds of pounds to escape, risking injury or damage to other crops. On the other hand, the legal rights of way must not be obstructed, and are supposed to be maintained in a usable condition. If you do come across any obstruction such as high brambles or stinging nettles, or fallen branches, then you may remove just sufficient of the obstruction or take the shortest possible diversion to enable you to pass, and the same applies to blockage by crops, locked gates or blocked stiles.

If a field across which a right of way runs is ploughed, the farmer is obliged to reinstate the line within two weeks, although this is not always done. The legal position is that the line of the right of way, as defined on the definitive map and normally as shown on OS maps, must be followed, even if your own inclination is to walk around the edge of the field. This is where a 1:25,000 scale map can prove so useful. If you do much walking in the country there will come a time when, possibly unintentionally, you find yourself on a track which is not a right of way. You may even be stopped by the owner who tells you that you are, in fact, trespassing. Do not argue. A polite apology, with an explanation as to how you made the mistake and a request for help, will often lead to an interesting conversation and suggestions as to the best way to go. In our experience in such situations, we always try to make the first approach if we meet someone, and we have never encountered any unpleasant consequences – quite the reverse, in fact. Of course the situation might be different if you were leading a large group of walkers instead of just enjoying an outing with your family or one or two like-minded companions, but the whole business comes down to mutual understanding of each other's position.

Signs may take many forms – a concrete marker in North Devon

How far?

The first thing to consider is the time available. Are you planning a short trip lasting perhaps two to three hours, say a morning or afternoon, or are you planning an all-day outing, or even longer? Whatever time you plan to take, it may not all be occupied in walking or riding. You may want to spend time visiting some place of interest, or in having a break for a meal, so take this into account before thinking of the distance you can cover. For afternoon or day trips remember that there will be fewer daylight hours during the winter.

A number of rules and formulae have been devised to determine the time required to walk various distances, the best-known of which is probably **Naismith's Rule**. However, so many factors come into the calculations that the situation tends to get out of hand. Walking on level unobstructed paths with firm surfaces can be very different from attempting a similar distance on muddy paths with stiles and gates, and the effect of hill slopes of varying steepness and length cannot be ignored. Remember that if several people are travelling together the time taken to pass over a stile can be quite significant compared to the time taken by one person, and the party will be delayed in consequence. The fitness and experience of all members of a party and the age of any children all add complications to the equation, so we can only suggest an approximate speed, to be modified to suit the circumstances. A reasonable pace for adults in small groups may be around 4 to 5 kilometres per hour plus extra time for any stiles, gates or other obstacles. When the route is hilly, add time for the uphill stretches, on a basis of 30 minutes for every 300m climbed. Small children and possibly pushchairs will obviously require extra time, but in any case do not over-estimate the distance you can do in the time available. On this basis a morning, afternoon or summer evening walk could be up to 10km in length, while up to 25km could be covered during a day; shorter hours of daylight in winter would limit this to around 15km. The object is to enjoy the experience, not to rush along as if you have a train to catch, so missing out on any views or interesting features. With experience you will soon get to know your own capabilities under different conditions.

Similar factors come into planning a cycle ride. There is little enjoyment to be found in gazing at the front wheel while pushing the pedals round as fast as possible. Take a relaxed and steady pace, allowing time to look about and enjoy the countryside, stopping from time to time for a break. A good average cruising speed on level roads would be around 20 kilometres per hour, and for route planning an average distance of 15km in each hour seems reasonable. Of course, extra hilly country or children in the party will affect the timing, and allowance for breaks for sight-seeing, snacks or meals should not be forgotten. When riding on bridleways or canal towpaths, a slower average speed can be expected.

Choosing a route

Decide the area you want to visit and the distance you can cover, then how you will get to the starting point. Next comes the question of how you will get back at the end of the walk or ride. The most interesting route is likely to be a circular one, unless public or other transport is available from the finish. Try to avoid having to return by the same route.

You may decide to use part or all of a waymarked route or one described in some other publication. Study your map beforehand. Often you can work out diversions to waymarked paths, even National Trails, which follow much more interesting and pleasant routes while still following rights of way. If your proposed route is a circular one, think if there is any advantage to be gained in following it in one direction or the other. Walking with the sun in your eyes, or against the wind, may lead you to choose the other way round. Try to climb the steepest hills early when you are fresh, and leave the easy bits until last. Study your map and think of where there may possibly be muddy areas in winter or bad weather. On very hot sunny days walking through woods may be preferable to walking uphill over open moorland, but remember the midges in the evenings under the trees or near lakes and streams!

If you plan a break for lunch, try to choose a suitable spot at a distance you will reach by the time you need it. Perhaps a pub, marked on the map, is your aim. If so, it might be advisable to check it is still in use as a pub. We have known cases where an isolated inn has closed since the map was published, so perhaps a phone call before leaving might save some disappointment.

Downland and farmland

Your earliest forays on foot are likely to be in less demanding country, following signed footpaths through woodland, fields and farmland. Your main problems are likely to be muddy tracks and missing signs, so your map will be useful. In wet weather or in low-lying ground bridleways and byways may be muddy due to use by horses or farm vehicles. In woodland or where tracks split, a compass can be useful even in this type of country, and you may encounter places where, for various reasons, tracks have been diverted and the actual situation on the ground doesn't agree with your map.

If you plan to follow footpaths which are shown on the map as rights of way but are not waymarked on the ground, a 1:25,000 scale map can be invaluable, as it can tell you which side of a hedge or fence the correct track runs. Nothing can be more frustrating than to follow the wrong side, only to find at the end that there is no gate or stile, so you have to retrace your steps.

Hills and moors

When planning a walk in hilly country or over open moorland, careful study of the map beforehand is even more important. There may be tracks or even rights of way shown, but in open country they may not always be easy to see on the ground and other tracks, not shown on the map, will add to the confusion. It will be worth drawing your proposed route in pencil on the map. When doing so, note any low-lying areas which may be boggy, and plan to avoid them. Watch, also, for indication of cliffs or crags, and plot your route to avoid these if possible. Note any prominent features such as Trig pillars, isolated trees or clumps, monuments, standing stones or stone crosses. All these make useful navigation marks. Cross streams by bridges if possible. Fords and stepping stones may be fine in dry weather, but in winter or after sudden summer storms they may prove quite impassable.

Awheel on a Dales Bridleway. (Derek Wood)

Route cards

Having decided where you want to go, it is useful to make some notes, even if only by marking in the proposed route on your map – using a soft pencil so it can be rubbed out afterwards. The alternative, to be recommended for any walk in hilly or open country, is to make a simple Route Card. Not only will this act as a useful guide for any tricky bits of navigation, but it can prove invaluable should you encounter bad weather during your journey.

When studying your map beforehand, note any places where extra care may be needed to find the correct route. Think of how poor visibility or bad weather might cause problems in route finding. As you follow the route on the map it naturally breaks down into stages, each with its own particular features and landmarks. Tracks through woodland or forest can be confusing, so even rough compass bearings can be helpful. In open country natural features such as prominent hill tops, dips in ridges, isolated rocky outcrops, and so on, make good aiming marks.

Having gone over the route in your mind, estimate the time required for each stage, based on the distances and amount of height gained and allowing for other difficulties, as described earlier in this chapter. Don't forget that your speed will be that of the slowest of your companions. Then within each section of the route, determine the bearings between prominent points or changes of direction. These will help keep you on your way, and can be very helpful if visibility deteriorates during your walk.

All this information then forms the basis for a simple route card, an example of which is shown on the next page. The plan is based on an actual walk covered by the OS Outdoor Leisure Map 28 Dartmoor. Estimated times allow for heights gained on each stage, but the whole route is fairly level. No allowance has been shown for a lunch break

How much detail you include on your Route Card is up to you, but it is a good idea to write it out clearly on a card and carry it in your map case where it is out of the rain but easily seen. Note on it any points which will be easy to identify on the ground to confirm your position, as this will save having to continually refer to the map.

Route Card: Gidleigh Church to Bellever YH

	Place & Grid Ref	*Bearing*	*Dist*	*Time*	*Remarks*
1	Start Gidleigh Ch. 671884		0	0	YH now closed
2	To: Entrance Gidleigh Park 672882		400m	6	Follow rd SE and left at junc
3	To: Exit Gidleigh Park 669873		1.5km	27	Follow Two Moors Way thro woods
4	To: Batworthy 662865	SW	1.1km	22	Follow rd to gateway
5	To: Batworthy Corner 660863	SW	400m	8	Follow track along wall to corner
6	To: Boundary Fernworthy Forest 652852	217°	1.4km	27	Across Shovel Down to forest boundary wall
7	To: Long Ridge 641844	SW	1.7km	26	Follow forest edge past two walls to gate
8	To: Grey Wethers 639832	188°	1.4km	25	Bridleway. Keep left of stream
9	To:Hartland Tor 640800	178°	3.2km	51	Bridleway. Cross two streams and keep close to river on right. Cross two walls
10	To: Ringhill Fm 647794	143°	1.1km	19	Bridleway on left of river then left to farm
11	To: Postbridge 649789	S x E	600m	10	Right on bridle-way to join road
12	To: Bellever YH 655774	SE	2km	34	Right along road over river. Left on bridleway to YH

Total Distance: 14.8km. Total time: 4hrs 15mins

Notes: Stage 6 – In poor visibility bearing from Batworthy Corner to Fernworthy Forest boundary wall should bring you to near the northern corner. Note the direction in which the wall runs to determine whether you have to retrace your steps to the corner, or continue SW along the wall to the gate into the forest.

Stage 8 – To Grey Wethers. The stones are just beyond where a wall is crossed by a stream, which should be on your right.

Stage 9 – If the bridleway is not easy to locate in bad visibility, keep to higher ground to left of bearing. A bearing of 164° from Grey Wethers to The Sheepfold (ruins), then 120° to Stannon, then farm track south to main road opposite the chapel at GR 652792, thence SW down road to Postbridge.

Allow extra time for finding gates/gaps in walls and for crossing streams.

Route plans for cycling

The same general ideas described for walkers apply to cyclists. Preliminary study of maps will show any very steep hills or tricky junctions with major roads, which you may wish to avoid. Suitable stops for refreshment and lunch may also be located in advance. When you have worked out the details, it is useful to prepare a route card in a similar way to that described for walkers, but less emphasis need be placed on Grid References and more on road or track junctions. Notes as to where roads go at junctions, found from your map, will be useful, as signposts at junctions will then help you to pinpoint your position without having to look at your map.

Useful information on your route card can include road numbers, where applicable, and which turning to take at cross-roads or T-junctions. Prominent features such as roundabouts, bridges, churches, and other landmarks which you can see without having to stop help to confirm your position.

Write the details clearly, in the order in which you will come to them, and place the card in your map holder, if you use one, so you can read it as you ride.

Keeping on track

Whether walking or cycling, be aware of exactly where you are as you go along. Look around you and note features which you can identify on the map. Obviously you know where you are when you start, then as you go along the way, keep a finger on the map and check frequently. Then if you come to a problem, you can easily refer to your last known point, not too far back, and check from there. If you think you have gone wrong, just stop and check where you might have gone wrong. Is the time you have taken realistic when related to the distance you think you have travelled? The map and your compass are probably much more reliable than your own 'built in' sense of direction, which is not as good as many people think.

CHAPTER FIVE

LOOKING AT THE WEATHER

A little light rain probably doesn't matter much if you are taking a short stroll in the park, and some snow can add a new dimension to many a walk in the country – provided it isn't blowing hard into your face! For many of us, however, living in towns and cities tends to shield us from the effects of weather, so it can come as something of a shock to find that out in the country things can be very different. If contemplating more extended trips it pays to be prepared for the worst, and even call off the planned journey if conditions are really bad. Up-to-date long and medium-range forecasts for the whole country or for specific regions are available in daily newspapers, on radio, on T.V., or by telephoning one of the numbers listed at the end of this chapter. National Park Information Centres often display local weather forecasts.

These sources of information are valuable for planning your journey, but British weather is known to be unpredictable. Someone once said that in the British Isles we don't have climate – only samples of weather! With its tendency to rapid change during a few hours or less, and the fact that the weather can be quite different in places only a short distance apart, it is useful to be able to anticipate those rapid changes which often occur, especially when walking in hilly country. In such circumstances it is not too much of an exaggeration to suggest this ability can make the difference between an enjoyable day out and a disaster. There are a number of signs which can help the walker and cyclist to make a reasonably accurate forecast, and some knowledge of what makes the weather what it is can be very useful.

The Weather Elements

The weather we experience at any given time and place is the result of complex interactions between a number of elements, such as atmospheric pressure, wind, temperature, humidity, and local geographical and other conditions.

Atmospheric Pressure

The pressure of the air upon the earth is measured by a barometer, calibrated either in inches representing the height of a column of mercury supported in a vertical open-ended tube, or nowadays in the scientific unit known as the *millibar* (mb). A pressure of 30 inches of mercury is equivalent to about 1016 mb, and this is the normal pressure at sea level. The atmospheric pressure varies with height above sea level; the higher you climb the lower the pressure, dropping to about 27 inches (914 mb) on top of a mountain 3000 ft (914m) high. For this reason any barometric pressure readings used in compiling weather maps or forecasts are always corrected to the equivalent sea-level values.

The pressure also varies with temperature. Warm air expands, becoming less dense and so exerting less pressure, and vice versa. On a weather map, points of equal (corrected) pressure may be linked with lines called *isobars*, similar in appearance to contour lines on a topographical map, so displaying areas of low and high pressure in a form useful to forecasters.

Wind

Wind is simply a movement of large masses of air from one area to another. Wind blows from a high pressure area towards an area of lower pressure, but the direction is modified by the earth's rotation. That explains the rule known to the weather men as Buys Ballot's Law, which simply says that when you stand with your back to the wind, the pressure will be lower on your left – that applies in the Northern Hemisphere. South of the Equator the rule is the opposite, but that need not concern us. The strength or force of the wind depends on how rapidly the pressure changes, and this can be seen from the plot of isobars on the weather map. In the same way that contours show how steep a slope is on the ground, so closely-spaced isobars show a steep pressure gradient, hence stronger winds. Taking into account the rule given above, inspection of the isobars can give a good idea of the likely strength and direction of the winds.

Wind direction is defined as the point of the compass *from* which the wind is blowing – a south-west wind is blowing *from* the south-west. Wind speed can be given in miles per hour, in knots (nautical miles per hour) or as a force on a scale of numbers from 0 to 12. This latter scale is known as the Beaufort Scale, devised originally in 1806 by Admiral Beaufort and based on the effect of the wind on sailing ships. A version suitably amended for use on land is given on the next page.

Beaufort Wind Scale

Force	*Wind speed (m.p.h)*	*Description*	*Observed effects on land*
0	0	Calm	Smoke rises vertically
1	1-3	Light air	Smoke drifts. Vanes still.
2	4-7	Light breeze	Wind felt on face. Vanes move. Leaves rustle
3	8-12	Gentle breeze	Leaves and twigs in motion. Light flags extended
4	13-18	Moderate breeze	Dust and loose paper move. Small branches move
5	19-24	Fresh breeze	Small trees in leaf sway. Wavelets on ponds & lakes
6	25-31	Strong breeze	Large branches move. Telephone wires hum
7	32-38	Moderate gale	Whole trees in motion.
8	39-46	Fresh gale	Twigs break off. Walking impeded
9	47-54	Strong gale	Slight damage to buildings. Slates & chimneys fall
10	55-63	Severe gale	Trees uprooted. Much damage to buildings.
11	64-75	Storm	Widespread damage.
12	Over 75	Hurricane	Devastation

Temperature

The temperature of still air close to the earth's surface depends on the intensity of sunlight reaching it, and is also affected by the surface conditions. Large land areas heat up and cool down quicker than large areas of water. Weather forecasts give the expected shade temperatures for *still air*, but we must not ignore the fact that the air temperature falls as you climb higher above sea level, the fall being around 3°C for every 1000 ft (300m) of ascent. This means that if the temperature at sea level is 15°C, a comfortable temperature for walking, when you climb 1000 feet it will drop to 12°C, and a further 1000 feet will bring a decidedly chilly 9°C. However, in real life we are very rarely concerned with still air, and the effects of wind lead to many complications.

Usually the higher you climb the stronger the wind, and this has an additional cooling effect on the body; the combined cooling effect of air temperature and wind speed is known as *wind chill*, and when conditions are wet it can be a cause of serious concern. As an example, if we take our previous figure of 12°C at 1000 feet, and a moderate breeze of 15mph (Force 4), the effective temperature would be approaching freezing. This factor needs taking into account even in summer when walking a relatively short distance up a hill from the safety of a car park in the valley.

Humidity

Relatively dry air passing over water or damp ground will soak up moisture like a sponge, and will hold this in the form of invisible water vapour. The amount of moisture held in this way depends on the temperature; the warmer the air the more moisture can be retained. When the temperature falls, the invisible water vapour condenses into droplets which form around the minute particles of dust always present in the atmosphere. In this way, clouds or mist and fog are produced.

Cooling of the moisture-laden air may come about through various effects, one of which is by convection. The air can be warmed by contact with the ground, resulting in rising currents. As the air rises it cools and if its temperature falls below the 'dew-point' or saturation temperature, clouds will form. Another common cause of cooling is the deflection of warm air by winds blowing against higher ground, so causing the air to rise.

Local variations

The interaction of all the above elements which combine to create our weather can be strongly influenced by local geographic features such as hills, valleys, lakes and sea. For example, the presence of hills and valleys may cause significant changes in local wind direction, and as we have seen, may also cause temperature changes leading to the formation of clouds. The temperature of the main body of air over a particular area may also be largely dependant on the ground conditions, such as large wooded areas or lakes, even by large built-up and industrial areas. For these reasons, general weather forecasts should always be supplemented by local information before coming to a conclusion which may decide for or against embarking on a trip.

Understanding the weather maps

Lows, highs, and fronts are all terms used on weather maps and in forecasts, so we should take a look at these to see what they mean. A 'low' refers to an area of low pressure, often called a depression. The isobars which depict this on the weather map will usually form enclosed loops around the centre point at which the pressure is lowest, and from what we have already said it follows that the winds will circulate in an anti-clockwise direction, towards the centre. At the centre the air will rise, gathering moisture which, on cooling, will form cloud, resulting in rain. Some indication of the wind strength will be given by the closeness of the isobars. Conversely, a 'high' is an area of high pressure, often termed an anticyclone, in which the winds circulate clockwise and cold air flows down and outwards. In real life things are never as simple as this. Usually there will be a complex system involving lows and highs with perhaps secondary centres and troughs and ridges, all of which make prediction of wind directions very complicated. As if that was not enough, depressions are usually associated with warm and cold 'fronts', which indicate where different air masses meet. A warm front is where the leading edge of a mass of warmer air meets colder air, and rises above it. As it rises so it becomes cooler and clouds form. The leading edge of a cooler air mass meeting warmer air forms a cold front, where there is a steeper boundary between the two masses, resulting in dense cloud and a shorter spell of very unsettled weather. Where warm and cold fronts merge, an 'occluded' front is said to form, leading to unstable, complex conditions. Figure 5.1 represents a typical weather map illustrating these features.

What to expect

Barometer readings

These can be useful, but of more significance to forecasting than the actual pressure is the *change* in pressure. Whilst a low reading, below say 1000 mb, is likely to be associated with cloudy conditions and rain, and a high reading of the order of 1050 mb with fine sunny weather, this can be misleading. A falling pressure probably denotes an approaching depression, which may mean that rain or cloudy weather on its way. On the other hand, a rising barometer reading in summer indicates a probable fine spell, although in winter it is likely to precede a fine day followed by a cold night, possibly with fog. A rapid *rate of change* in pressure probably indicates that the current conditions may soon change, and a slow steady change will be followed by a more prolonged stable period.

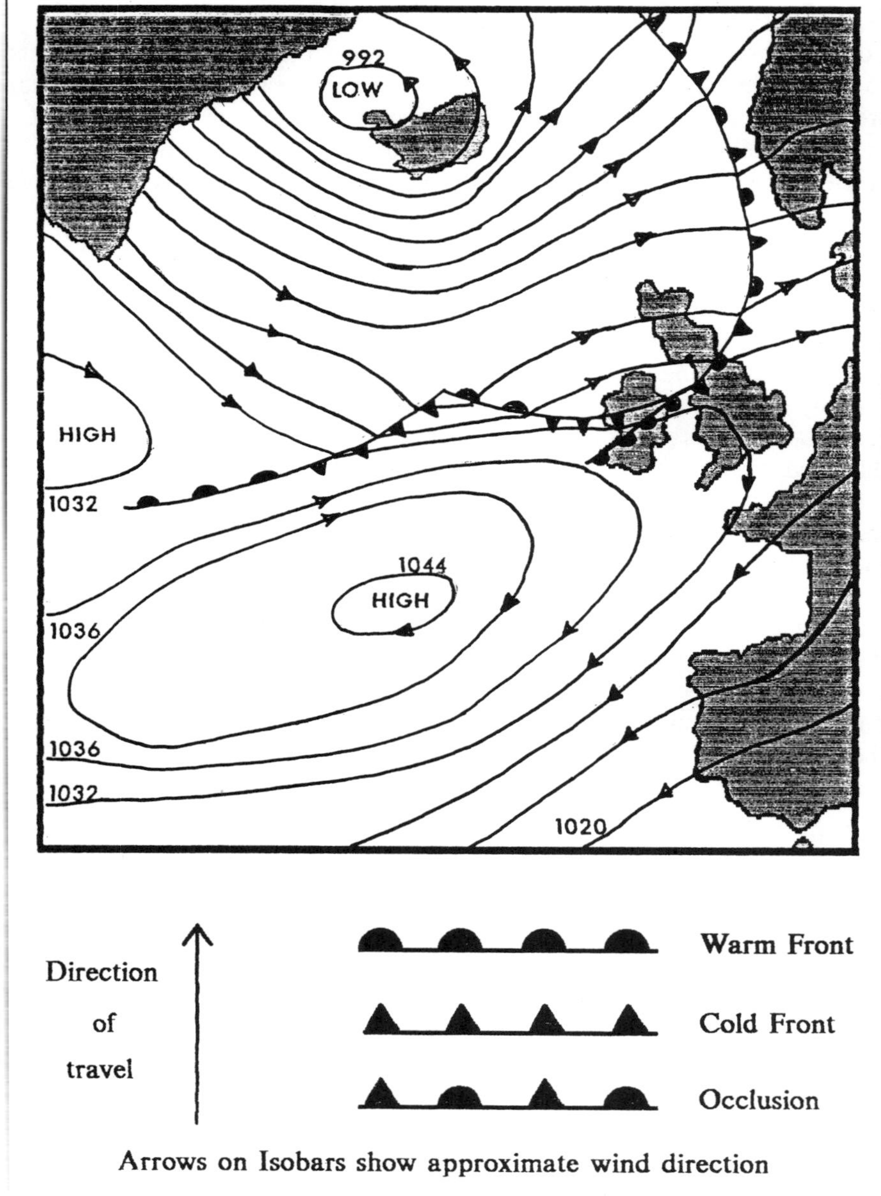

Fig 5.1. A typical weather map

Clouds

Watching the clouds can often give clues as to what to expect. Wind blowing against a ridge of high ground will rise, so becoming cooler, and cloud may form.

If the cloud is low, rain or drizzle is likely on the side facing the wind, and if really low there may be hill fog. Once the air has passed over the crest it will sink, becoming warmer, and the cloud will disperse. Often there will be bright sunshine on the sheltered lee side of high ground.

The type and height of clouds can tell us a great deal about present and future conditions. Very high wispy white clouds resembling feathers are *cirrus* clouds, composed of ice crystals rather than water droplets. They are often present during spells of fine weather, although when they are first seen approaching from the south-west they are often an early warning of rain to come (Figure 5.2).

Fig 5.2. Cirrus cloud

Cirro-cumulus clouds, often referred to as a 'mackerel sky', appear as lines or ripples of white high in the sky and may warn of unsettled showery weather, possibly with an increase in wind within a few hours (Figure 5.3).

Fig 5.3. Cirro-cumulus cloud

Another high-level cloud formation is *cirro-stratus* which appears as a thin white veil covering the sky. It is formed of ice crystals and often causes a halo around the sun or, at night, a ring around the moon. With a falling barometer the probability is for wind and rain to come. At middle levels, *alto-stratus* clouds form a grey veil over the sky through which the sun or moon may appear like watery discs. Rain, or if cold enough, snow will be likely. A more welcome sign may be the approach of *alto-cumulus* clouds, comprising layers or masses of cloud, dark on their lower parts and throwing shadows on the ground (Figure 5.4).

Fig 5.4. Alto-cumulus cloud

These may appear when bad weather is clearing and the sun begins to break through. At the lowest levels, *cumulus* clouds can be likened to a pile of cotton wool with a flat base. The small ones which drift slowly across the sky often promise fine weather (Figure 5.5).

Fig 5.5. Cumulus cloud

The bigger ones, on the other hand, foretell sudden heavy showers separated by fair periods. If the larger clouds are seen to reduce in size and break up this indicates a probable improvement in the weather, whilst if they grow in size and number wet or unsettled conditions are likely. *Cumulo-nimbus* clouds are bigger and much darker, and often develop from a low level into huge towering masses, perhaps flattening out at the top into an anvil shape. These are thunder clouds bringing heavy rain or hail, and possibly thunder and strong gusty wind (Figure 5.6).

Fig 5.6. Cumulo-Nimbus cloud

The grey sky associated with continuous falling rain or snow is covered by a nearly uniform dark grey layer of *nimbo-stratus* cloud below which there may be ragged trailing 'scud'. A uniform layer of cloud called *stratus* looks like fog but is clear of the ground, producing drizzle and poor visibility. Stratus can form very quickly and may develop into hill fog and deteriorating conditions when the barometer is falling. However, in summer, low-lying stratus often disperses as the sun warms the air, leading to a fine day. Finally, a cloudless sky will allow the sun to raise the temperature of the ground and the air above during the day, although an increase in dust and water vapour in the air may reduce visibility. At night, the absence of cloud normally leads to a cold night, with frost in winter.

The wind

In the British Isles the prevailing wind is from the south-west, bringing clouds and rain from the Atlantic in winter and generally milder conditions. South-east winds from the Continent will be warm and dry in summer but bitterly cold in winter. North-east winds are also likely to bring cold air from northern Europe and Scandinavia, while sharp squalls with heavy rain showers separated by bright intervals are often associated with a north-west wind. However, as we have already pointed out, this general trend can be modified by local conditions. One feature to be found near the coast is the cycle of land and sea breezes. During the day the land warms up quicker than the sea, so the air above land rises, causing a breeze to blow in from the sea – a sea breeze which will be cool because it has blown over the cooler water. At night, the land cools quicker than the water and the situation is reversed. It is possible for these effects to overcome the prevailing wind over land, so giving quite a localised weather pattern. Wind is said to be *backing* when its direction changes in an anti-clockwise direction, and to be *veering* when changing in a clockwise direction. Ahead of a depression the wind backs and increases in strength, while it veers when a front passes. The veering wind may decrease in strength although there may be squalls.

Thunder and Lightning

A thunder storm is perhaps the most spectacular and to some the most frightening aspect of our weather. Thunder itself is only noise, and cannot harm anyone. In fact, when you hear the sound, the lightning discharge which caused it has already "been and come and gone" as they say! The continuous rumbling over a period of time is simply the result of the initial sound reverberating backwards and forwards between clouds, buildings and the ground. A sharp 'clap' of thunder originates from a fairly near lightning discharge, whilst the long drawn out rumbling comes from more distant flashes. It is possible to estimate the distance away that the actual lightning flash occurred by noting the time between seeing the flash and hearing the first sound. As a rough guide, five seconds delay represents about one mile.

From a weather point of view, thunder storms are areas of extremely turbulent air existing within large cumulo-nimbus clouds which can reach to great heights. Without going into the details, many of which are still not well understood, very high electrical voltages are induced within the cloud and these high voltages discharge to points of opposite polarity within the cloud or on the ground as lightning. A lightning discharge is, in fact, a series of arcs travelling backwards and forwards, all taking place within a fraction of a second. Often there will be a strong wind ahead of an approaching thunder storm, blowing towards the base of the cloud, and very heavy rain or hail can commonly occur. Depending on the prevailing conditions, the storm may be very localised, with neighbouring areas still enjoying sunshine, or several storms may combine, drifting across country for several hours. We will consider the best action to take if caught in a thunderstorm when dealing with safety in Chapter Seven.

A general summary

The following rough guide to what you may expect may be of help if you cannot obtain more accurate local forecasts; the more signs you can observe the better your predictions, but remember local conditions can have a marked effect.

Wet and unsettled weather may be indicated by a rapidly falling barometer, increase in size and number of small clouds, changing from cirrus to the lower cumulo-nimbus, with anvil tops warning of possible thunder. Rain will be almost certain to follow a backing wind from the south-west, especially with thickening cloud. A red sky in the morning or yellow at sunset, and no dew are all warning signs of bad weather to come.

Fair weather is indicated by a steadily rising barometer and breaking and thinning cloud, particularly cumulus or stratus. A clear sky foretells frost. Wind veering to the north-east suggests cold and dry conditions, and a red sky at sunset with heavy dew are both indicators of a fine day to come.

A useful indication of future developments in the weather is the so-called *crossed winds rule.* Wind direction near the ground may differ from that at higher altitudes, as indicated by the movement of high clouds, and this latter wind is generally responsible for the movement of depressions. To apply the rule, stand with your back to the lower wind, making sure you have the true direction, unaffected by local ground features. (The lowest clouds may give an indication of true low wind direction). Then observe the direction in which the highest clouds are moving. The rule is as follows:

> With your back to the lower wind, if the upper wind comes from your left, deteriorating weather is likely.
>
> With your back to the lower wind, if the upper wind comes from your right, an improvement in weather is likely.
>
> With your back to the lower wind, if the upper wind blows from behind you or ahead of you, little change is likely.

Some popular beliefs and sayings

Over the years, people whose livelihood and even safety depended on the weather devised many beliefs and sayings relating to present and future weather conditions. Sailors, of course, had more than a casual interest in the weather, as did farmers and others living and working in the country.

Although many of these beliefs do not stand up to careful investigation, there remains a large body of 'weather lore' which is at least as reliable as some of the more scientific forecasts we get today, mainly because they rely on localised experience. We offer a selection of some of the better known sayings and beliefs, and you may like to test them for yourselves:

Fine before seven, rain by eleven

Red sky in the morning, shepherd's warning
Red sky at night, shepherd's delight

When the dew is on the grass rain will never come to pass
When grass is dry at morning light look for rain before the night

Come the wind before the rain be ready to make sail again
Come the rain before the wind then your sheets and halyards mind

When the distant view is clear rain will very soon be here

Nature's forecasters

Animals and birds react quickly to changes in the weather and seem to be able to tell what changes are in the offing. Sheep always feed on the windward side of a hill, so if they move around to the other side you can be certain of a change coming. Cows are more troubled by stinging insects just before rain, so flicking tails against their sides is a sign rain is on its way. Rooks feeding near their rookeries foretell wet and windy weather, and gulls fly inland when it is rough on the coast. Swallows fly high in fine weather, but when they dip low rain is coming. Often before a storm, birds become uncannily quiet.

Trees and shrubs in exposed positions lean away from the prevailing wind, so you can tell at a glance the direction from which the wind normally blows.

Information sources

Newspapers

The better class papers include weather maps are useful for general trends over the next 24 – 48 hours covering the country as a whole.

Television

In addition to the forecasts which follow the National and Regional news transmissions on the BBC and ITV channels, both services have fairly detailed coverage on their respective text transmissions, namely BBC 1 & 2 Ceefax, both on page 400, and ITV Teletext on page 180. The latter service includes rather more detail and has short term and regional forecasts.

Radio

BBC Radio 2 and Radio 4 carry forecasts at intervals during the day, starting at around 6am. In addition, a wide selection of local BBC and Independent radio stations carry local forecasts. Details of frequencies of National and Local radio stations for each area are given in the Place Names Index annex to each map in the O.S. Travelmaster series.

Telephone

Current and expected weather details from the appropriate Met Office Weather Centre. The numbers are on the O.S. Travelmaster maps.

The 'Weathercall' service has recorded local and regional forecasts for the next few hours and trends for up to 48 hours. The number to call for each area is as follows:

0891-505- plus the area number –

National	300	Dyfed & Powys	314
Greater London	301	Gwynedd & Clwyd	315
Kent, Surrey & Sussex	302	NW England	316
Dorset, Hants & IOW	303	W & S Yorks	317
Devon & Cornwall	304	NE England	318
Wilts, Gloucs, Avon & Som.	305	Cumbria & Lake Dist.	319
Berks., Bucks. & Oxon.	306	SW Scotland	320
Herts., Beds. & Essex	307	Glasgow & Strathclyde	321
Norfolk, Suffolk & Cambs.	308	Edin,S Fife,Loth.& Brdrs	322
Glamorgan & Gwent	309	E Central Scotland	323
Salop, Hereford & Worcs.	310	Grampian & E Highlands	324
Central Midlands	311	NW Scotland	325
E Midlands	312	Caithness Ork. & Shet.	326
Lincs & Humberside	313	N Ireland	327

These recorded messages pack a lot of information into a short time and you may find it difficult to note down all the details. They are also not free and, particularly at Peak Call Rate, you may need to have plenty of change available if using a call box.

CHAPTER SIX

HEALTH AND FIRST AID

The right type of food

In order to function properly and remain healthy, the body needs sufficient quantities of the right type of food, but the balance of these types must also be correct. Food consists of protein for tissue growth and muscle repair, fats in small quantities to provide warmth, carbohydrates to produce energy, minerals such as calcium for healthy teeth and bone tissue, and iron to produce red blood cells. It has been increasingly recognised that fibre is an important part of our diet as it provides roughage and keeps our insides working properly. Vitamins are essential to our good health, and water is necessary to replace fluids lost by normal physiology and by physical exertion. Proteins take about four hours to be absorbed by the body, thus producing energy at a much slower rate than carbohydrates, which are assimilated easily and quickly converted into energy. Surplus carbohydrate will be converted into fat, helping to provide warmth. If we have too much fat and do not work it off, it will be stored by the body, giving us extra weight to carry which we do not need.

The golden rule for a good day out is to start with a good breakfast with a high carbohydrate content, including both sugars and starches. The starches and fibre will fill you up and keep you going, and the sugars will give you instant energy. Muesli cereals, wheat flakes, bran, etc, with the addition of a banana and some brown sugar is a good start.

These will give you the energy you need at the beginning of the day. There is nothing wrong with a bacon and egg breakfast provided that you also include some cereal and/or wholemeal bread, to give you the carbohydrate and fibre. The proteins will then be available to give you extra energy mid-morning.

Protein foods include eggs, meat, fish, cheese and milk. All contain some fat as well as the vital minerals we need in our diet. The approximate daily requirement for a balanced diet is sixty per cent carbohydrate, twenty per cent protein and twenty per cent fat.

It is important to have sufficient Vitamin B because the body uses this to convert your carbohydrate intake into sugars (for energy). It can be found in wholemeal bread, yeast extract, lean meat, liver, fruit and nuts. Vitamin C must be taken daily, and is found in fresh citrus fruits, green salads and green vegetables.

Energy

A Kilo-calorie (normally known simply as a Calorie) is the unit used to measure the heat-producing power of food; in other words, the energy power. Food labelling is now so comprehensive that most packets and tins have a table listing the energy value of the contents, the amount of carbohydrate, protein and fat contained, etc. The average adult male needs a thousand calories per day just to keep his body functioning when at rest. On average, a healthy adult male will require about 2000 calories a day, and a woman about 1500 calories a day for normal activities. A gentle walk or cycle ride will not involve the use of a lot of extra energy, but more strenuous walks and rides will use up a great deal. It follows that, on such trips, your normal daily intake of calories will need to be increased, and if you are on a longer trip, perhaps backpacking or cycle-camping, carrying heavy loads, you will need even more energy to keep you going. When very active, you may need as much as 3500 calories, or even more, depending on your age, sex and build and the actual amount of energy being used by the body.

Energy sometimes needs replenishing fast, especially after a steep climb up a hill, for example. So what you eat is important. One gramme of carbohydrate and one gramme of protein each produce 4.1 Calories. We have already said that carbohydrates take less time to be assimilated into the body, and this applies particularly to sugars. It follows that to replace lost energy quickly, you should eat plenty of carbohydrates. If you do not have enough to eat, your blood sugar can drop rapidly; your legs will feel like jelly, as if they cannot support you, and you could break out into a cold sweat. Cyclists call this 'the bonk', but it can happen to walkers, too. The best cure is not to let it happen, but if it does, stop and rest, chew a glucose sweet or a Dextrosol tablet, followed by a muesli bar or something similar. A good general rule to follow is to stop before you become tired, eat as soon as you are hungry, or before, and drink in small quantities when you are thirsty.

Food on the journey

Many people like to plan for a mid-day stop for lunch at a pub or similar establishment, to rest their legs and replenish lost energy. Many years back, when walking in Norfolk, we decided to do just that, and arrived at the pub, clearly marked on an up-to-date map, to find boarded windows and no sign of life anywhere! A little further on we found a garage which sold cold drinks, but no food. Since then, we have always carried sufficient food to keep us going. Once caught out, it never happens again. We have also found pubs displaying large 'pub food' signs which do not serve food midday at weekends! Of course, if you are walking somewhere you know, where there is a choice of pubs, O.K., but we think it best to be prepared So, do you choose sandwiches or 'Trail snacks'?

Mars bars are a quick way of providing replacement energy. The mini-Mars bars can be useful, as you will not always need a full-sized bar to revive you. A supply of muesli bars, obtainable from Health food shops and many supermarkets make a good, healthy alternative to chocolate. They don't melt in hot sun and are convenient to carry in the pocket of your rucksack or cycle bag. Add some raisins in a little plastic pot, and maybe some ready-to-eat washed dried apricots or prunes, plus perhaps an apple, and you have some good trail food. Some walkers like to eat little and often, say a muesli bar every hour, while others prefer just a mid-morning snack and a packed lunch at mid-day. You will have your own preferences for sandwich fillings, but we usually make ours from three or four rounds of wholemeal bread, with cheese and Marmite, pickle, or sliced tomato, or sometimes ham with curd cheese, and occasionally egg and tomato. All these will provide a substantial lunch, to which we normally add an apple or banana. This will give you the energy you need for the rest of the day. Do not eat too much at lunchtime, or you will find it very uncomfortable walking or cycling on an over-full stomach. It is not a bad idea to eat your sandwiches at lunchtime, and stop again mid-afternoon and eat the fruit.

Drinks

Some kind of drink should always be carried. In summer, many will carry a fruit drink, or even water, but fizzy drinks should be avoided. They do not refresh you, and can leave a bloated feeling in the stomach, not ideal for walking or cycling. For the same reason, if you stop at a pub, don't overdo the beer. You must ensure that your fluid intake is sufficient to replace that lost by physical exertion. You may lose several pounds of body weight, as well as valuable mineral salts in this manner, especially if you are cycling in hot weather. Some specialist high-energy drinks can be obtained which help to replace mineral salts lost through sweating, as well as being refreshing. It is important to drink enough in hot weather, and little and often rather than taking great draughts now and again is the rule. Do not drink quantities of very cold water, especially in very hot weather, and do not drink from streams.

Getting into trim

To keep fit it is necessary not to overstretch yourself. If you are not used to walking or cycling long distances it is absolutely essential to start slowly, walking or cycling for short distances and gradually increasing these as time goes on. If you try and do a long walk or cycle ride when you are unused to doing so you are likely to become exhausted and be a nuisance to your companions. It follows that you must keep fit.

You could do this by joining a keep-fit or aerobics class, or do some exercises with a video or TV celebrity, or try an exercise bike. But there is no need to spend out on such things when you can keep fit by climbing the stairs at work instead of using the lifts or escalator, and walk or cycle to the local shops instead of popping down in the car! If your main shopping centre is, say, three or four miles from your home, why not walk in, using footpaths if you can, and come back on the bus with your shopping? All simple and cheap ways of keeping fit.

Your feet must be well cared for, especially if backpacking, as carrying a heavy pack will impose a lot of strain on them – its weight presses down, causing movement in the bones of the feet, and making them swell. In hot weather they will sweat profusely, causing great discomfort inside your boots unless you are careful. Prepare your feet properly before setting out, and you will have few problems. You might get a small blister at first, but go without preparing your feet and you are courting trouble. Put on your boots and go for some short walks, starting on tarmac pavements or lanes. Although this will be harder on the feet than grass, it helps to break the boots in quickly. Watch out for any 'hot spots' or redness which will lead to a blister, and treat accordingly. Before embarking on a backpacking trip, harden your feet, even if you normally have no problems with blisters. Wash and dry your feet thoroughly every night, then rub a little surgical spirit into your heels, massaging the ball of the heel as well as the back by the Achilles tendon. Treat the soles of your feet in the same way, and along the sides of the big toes. Finish by dusting your feet with a quality foot powder.

After this preparation, take some regular walks in your new boots, until you can walk about eight miles without discomfort, then start carrying a rucksack, gradually increasing your load to what you will have to carry for the time you plan to be away. It may seem like a lot of unnecessary time and trouble, but this preparation will add a great deal to your enjoyment when you finally start real backpacking.

It is a good idea to keep your body weight within sensible limits, and you certainly should try not to be overweight, or you will tire quickly and have no energy. Your heart will be working quite hard, whether you are cycling or walking, especially when you have to climb a steep hill, so don't make it harder for yourself by carrying more bodyweight than you need! If it is necessary to reduce your weight, talk to your doctor who will be able to advise you. Don't diet unnecessarily!

The main thing to remember is that if you eat the right type of food, in the right quantities, and take regular exercise, you will be fit enough to walk or cycle wherever you wish to go.

First Aid

Your personal first-aid kit

Never go out without some kind of first aid kit. It need not be elaborate, and we hope you do not have to use it, but always be prepared for the eventuality. We have found that we have rarely had to use our first aid kits except to help someone else! Cuts and grazes, stings, (both from insects and plants), insect bites and splinters are all hazards which you may come across in the outdoors. Your first aid kit should contain the necessary items to deal with these problems. Carry some kind of antiseptic wipes for cleaning cuts and grazes. Do not carry creams as they do not cleanse the wound. Adhesive plaster dressings are a 'must' – probably the most useful is a waterproof strip dressing which can be cut to size. A small pair of folding scissors will deal with the problem. Very small individual plasters are useful for cuts on fingers. Melolin sterilised dressings are useful for larger wounds which need to be kept clean, and can be held on the skin with zinc oxide plaster. For a really deep wound, a plain dressing which comes attached to its own bandage and is sterile until opened is a useful standby. We have had to use such a dressing only once in over twenty years, but we were glad we had it with us. Anti-histamine sting-relief cream or 'Wasp-Eeze' spray in a small aerosol pack are useful for dealing with stings of all kinds. Insect-repellent, either 'wipes' packed in idividual sachets, or a stick, gel or spray will keep away mosquitoes, midges and other flying horrors. A crepe bandage or elasticated support might be useful if you are unfortunate enough to turn your ankle or twist your knee, and these should be considered essential in hilly country or on extended trips. Remember that the wet grass on the steep scarp slopes of the downs can cause you to slip and twist your ankle just as easily as scree on a mountain path.

A crewel needle threaded with darning wool and a fine sewing needle are useful for dealing with blisters, splinters and thorns.

You should also carry a few pain-killers *for your own use only*. Take what you normally prefer to use so that if you do need them they are available. *Never* give any pain-killers to those who are not members of your immediate family and whose medical history you do not know.

We suggest you make up a kit to suit your own preferences, packed into a small plastic container or wallet. If you buy a ready-made kit, get it from a reputable supplier, check the contents carefully, and do not hesitate to replace unsuitable or unwanted items with those of your own choosing. The following items are suggested for a basic kit:

1 waterproof strip dressing, 60mm x 150mm
6 individual Band-Aid or similar adhesive dressings
1 Melolin non-adherent dressing, 50mm x 50mm
3 antiseptic wipes (sachets)
1 sterilised medium plain dressing
1 small roll zinc oxide plaster, 12mm wide
1 book of matches
1 small sewing needle
1 crewel needle, threaded with darning wool
2-4 pain-killers, foil wrapped
1 small pack of Moleskin, or Compeed plasters
Folding scissors
Insect repellent
1 tube sting relief or 'Waspeeze'
Safety pins
Tweezers

You should also consider including the following:

1 crêpe bandage, 75mm wide
1 triangular bandage
Sun protection cream
Calamine lotion
Lip salve
1 large Melolin dressing 100mm x 100mm
Glucose tablets

Dealing with minor accidents and illness

Burns and scalds are nasty at any time, and there is always the risk of hot tea or coffee spilled from a flask causing injury. If you are camping on an extended trip, there is the risk of burns from stoves and hot pans. The remedy is to cool the area with plenty of cold water as quickly as possible; limbs can be plunged into a bucket or a stream. Keep the affected area wet and get medical attention for the casualty as soon as you can. Burns and scalds cause a sudden major loss of body fluid, causing shock. Keep the patient warm and give warm, sweet drinks, but do not overheat him. If possible, keep him lying still whilst help is fetched.

Insect bites and stings are best treated with an anti-histamine cream or one of the pocket sprays such as 'Waspeeze', which is very effective. Nettle stings can be treated in the same manner, but the old fashioned remedy of putting a dock leaf on the affected area works very well.

If stung by a bee, try to remove the sting with tweezers or a needle, but do not squeeze it or you will pump the poison into the wound. Once the sting is out, put some anti-histamine cream on the site.

Blisters can be prevented by applying moleskin plasters to unbroken, sensitive areas, or you can use one of the special cushioned pads now available, such as 'Compeed'. Treat a blister by sterilising a crewel needle in a match flame, then push it gently through the blister from one side to the other. If the needle is threaded with a piece of darning wool, pull it slowly through and it will soak up the fluid before applying a plaster. This old-fashioned remedy works very well in relieving the pressure and pain.

A fine sewing needle can be sterilised in a match flame and used to remove splinters or small thorns if you cannot grip them with tweezers.

Too much sun can cause problems, so make sure the body is well ventilated in hot weather by wearing sufficient loose clothing. Wear a sun hat, and keep your neck and shoulders covered. Drink plenty of fluids before setting out for the day, and drink little and often during the day. Drink slowly in hot weather. Those with sensitive skins should use protective cream with a high ultra-violet inhibiting factor, which should be applied frequently. Too much ultra-violet light can cause sun-rash, which is very irritating. This can be soothed by an application of calamine lotion or after-sun preparation. Prickly heat, caused by profuse sweating, consists of a rash of minute blisters and can be relieved by bathing with a weak solution of bicarbonate of soda in water. Remember that the sun's rays will penetrate even through a cloudy sky in summer, and if you are up in the hills or near water the risk of sunburn is greater. Sunburn prevents the sweat glands from functioning properly, so the body becomes overheated. If you become burned, treat by gently pouring cold water over the affected area. Medical help should be sought in severe cases, and particularly if a child is affected. If you become tired and giddy on a very hot day, stop and rest for a while, in the shade, and take frequent sips of water. A glucose sweet may help to overcome any nausea. If necessary, cut short your walk or ride and return home at a leisurely pace.

The effect of strong winds can be quite severe at any time of the year. If you are in the hills, or even on the downs, strong winds can cause windburn. A light application of lipsalve will prevent your lips becoming cracked and sore. Do this also in very hot or very cold weather. If your skin is very sensitive, use protective cream, such as that supplied for skiers, on your face.

Warning signs of trouble

What to do and what not to do

No one expects to get anything but enjoyment out of a day's walk or cycle ride. The element of risk is fundamental to all outdoor activities, so be prepared to help yourself or your companions if your luck runs out whilst you are out in the countryside. Do learn the basic principles of first aid so that you can deal with minor injuries and how to cope with more serious accidents and emergencies. You may never find yourself in such a situation, but remember that even a small graze or scratch, or a minor burn caused by touching a hot pan, can spoil your own enjoyment.

It is wise to observe your companions, because the unexpected can happen. If a person suddenly becomes morose or irritated, or behaves irrationally, there is something wrong. It may simply be that he or she is over-tired and needs to rest, even though that person may deny it. The immediate answer is for everyone to take a rest, but continue to observe behaviour, because it could be an early warning of a heart attack. If you suspect that this may be the case, particularly if your companion has chest pains or is breathless, get help immediately by dialling 999 from the nearest phone.

Irrational behaviour in very cold weather or in the high hills could mean that person is beginning to suffer from exposure. Indeed, symptoms of exposure can be seen in ordinary open country, when people go out without sufficient clothing, or incorrect clothing for the time of year.

Dealing with exposure and other major emergencies is covered in more detail in Chapter Seven.

A bad fall from a cycle or a badly twisted ankle, or even a broken limb can happen. Here again, get help as soon as possible. Do not move a casualty who cannot feel his legs after an accident, as this is a sign of spinal injury and permanent damage could result. If on a road, direct any traffic around the person until the ambulance arrives.

This is not a first aid manual. The best way to learn first aid is through the local Red Cross or St John's Ambulance societies, who normally run courses for the general public, although a small fee may be charged. Some hospitals organise sessions to teach people the warning signs of a heart attack, and what to do if you think someone is having one.

This chapter is intended to let you know that illness and accidents can happen, not that they will. At least we have tried to tell you what to do if they do occur, although we hope very much that they do not.

CHAPTER SEVEN

SAFE AND SOUND

Any outdoor activity can involve certain risks, but if we stay at home statistics show that is the environment in which the majority of personal accidents occur. The answer is to go out, enjoy yourself, but take sensible precautions.

Safety on the road

Walking

There are times when you have to walk along a road. If there is a footpath, use it. If the road is a busy one, walk away from the edge of the path to avoid the slipstream from big fast vehicles. Keep small children beside you, away from the roadway. If necessary, hold their hand or even keep them on a rein. Where there is no footpath, walk in single file on the right, facing the oncoming traffic, keeping children between adults. The only exception to keeping to the right may be where there is a bend. In this case it may be safer to walk on the opposite side of the road so you are more easily seen by oncoming traffic.

- ❐ If you have to cross a road, especially a busy one, use a crossing, footbridge or subway, or cross at traffic lights. Where this is not possible, choose a point with good visibility in both directions, such as a straight stretch or at the crest of a rise. Keep a good lookout for approaching traffic, and when clear, cross all members of your group together as quickly as possible.
- ❐ When approaching a road from a footpath, take great care before emerging onto the road, looking both ways for approaching vehicles. Remember that cycles can approach quickly but silently.
- ❐ When several walkers are following a road in single file, the backmarker should shout a warning of approaching vehicles from behind, and the warning should be passed on if the group occupies a long stretch of road.
- ❐ At unmanned rail crossings take extra care, looking and listening before attempting to cross. Small children should be carried if necessary.
- ❐ If, through unexpected delays or other reasons, you have to walk along a

road after dark, at least the leader and backmarker of the party should wear or carry some reflective or light-coloured clothing or other article, and use a torch to indicate their presence on the approach of a vehicle – but do not flash torches upwards or towards the vehicle driver. The same applies if other walkers approach. There is nothing more annoying than to have a torch flashed into your eyes.

- If rain is falling, take extra care. Drivers will have more difficulty in seeing you, and with the hood of your waterproof jacket up, you will have difficulty in hearing vehicles approaching from behind.

Cycling

Safe cycling depends on meeting legal requirements and using common sense and courtesy towards other people.

Good brakes and good lights are, of course, legal requirements. Make sure your lights are in good working order, and use them! This applies particularly to the early evenings when dusk is falling. You may still be able to see, but can you be seen? Misty and rainy weather conditions can be particularly hazardous. Also, make sure your lights are not partly obscured by any panniers or other bags you have on your bike.

- The Highway Code contains much information relating to cycles and safety. Make sure you are familiar with it. The question of helmets has been mentioned in Chapter Two, and again in Chapter Eight with reference to children. The decision is yours.

- Wear reflective bands or clothing to increase your visibility. It is a good idea to have reflective patches on the back of panniers or saddle bags, and in Chapter Eight we mentioned the little 'flags' on vertical wands on childrens' bikes.

- If riding in a group, do not ride more than two abreast, and only if the road is suitable. When traffic approaches from behind, move into single file. If the road is very narrow, pull into a suitable gate entrance or other place and let it pass.

- When riding in single file, keep children between adult riders. If riding two abreast, children should be on the inside.

- Remember that your machine is almost silent, so pedestrians ahead of you may not know you are coming. A short 'ping' on your bell in good time will warn them without scaring them.

- Where there is a suitable cycle path, use it. Unfortunately, many such paths are obstructed by parked vehicles, or are covered with litter, including broken glass, so this may not be a good option.
- Country lanes may offer the hazard of hedge trimmings. Although it is illegal to leave these lying on the road, the odd hawthorn twig can play havoc with your tyres.
- When riding with full camping kit, remember the stopping power of your brakes will be reduced, especially if the ground is wet.
- On bridleways and shared paths, cycles should give way to pedestrians, and to horse riders.

Safety in the countryside

Footpaths through fields, farms, streams and rivers, lakes and duck ponds, trees and woods, all offer delights and hazards, particularly when taking children out in the country.

Brambles and stinging nettles can cause very uncomfortable scratches or rashes, but they are not particularly dangerous. Hawthorn or blackthorn hedge cuttings on the ground, however, have very long sharp thorns which can easily penetrate thin shoes and give a very nasty injury to a foot if trodden on. Ripe blackberries are very tempting, but many equally attractive-looking fruits and berries in the hedgerows are not only unpleasant; some are definitely poisonous. Children can be taught that even birds would be ill if they ate some berries. Yew and laurel are especially dangerous. The sap of some plants can have serious effects on sensitive skin if handled, and unless you are really expert, fungus is best left well alone. In Chapter Six we described how to deal with insect stings and bites.

The surroundings of farms are often littered with debris in the form of abandoned farm machines, very fascinating to children. Keep away, as some can be dangerous if climbed on. Also, on a working farm keep clear of tractors and other appliances. The drivers cannot always see a person standing close, and the noise of the engines prevents them hearing. Beware of barbed wire and electric fences; rusty barbed wire can inflict quite nasty scratches. A hot day makes a paddle, or even a swim in a stream very tempting, but do make sure first that it is not too deep and that the bottom is not deep in mud. The same applies to lakes and ponds. Such waters can also be very cold and the resulting shock could have dangerous consequences. Never be tempted to drink water from a stream or river, no matter how hot the day.

Children love climbing trees, but old oaks and ashes in particular have a habit of shedding branches, with possibly disastrous results to anyone climbing them or standing nearby.

Safety on moorland and in the hills

It is very inadvisable to walk alone in such country as accidents can happen no matter how careful you are. On the other hand, groups of over ten people can be dangerous as it is not easy to keep them all together in difficult situations. The recommended size of party for walking in the hills is from three to six, and the party should remain together at all times. The only exception to this is in case of accident, when someone has to go for help. We deal with this aspect later.

What to take

In addition to your map, compass and route card, carry a whistle and a good torch, and note details of any mountain rescue posts or information centres in the area, and possible locations of telephones in villages or farms.

When walking in open hilly country the importance of good clothing and footwear cannot be over-emphasised. No matter how fine and warm the weather may be at your start, extra warm and waterproof garments should be carried, and if you do not plan to camp, each member of the party should have a bivvy bag or survival bag and a piece of closed-cell foam mat. The survival bag is simply a large plastic bag with which your whole body can be covered from your feet to above your shoulders. The mat provides insulation from the cold ground if you want to sit for a meal break. Other uses will be described later.

Some emergency rations such as muesli bars, chocolate, dates, Kendal Mint Cake, crispbread and cheese, together with provision for something to drink should not be forgotten. A small stove and pan together with the means of making a hot drink and/or soup take little space in your kit. It may not be necessary to carry water in country where streams are present, but do carry a few water purifying tablets. Boiling water for a sufficient time to ensure its purity takes time and fuel. You may be short of the former, and you have to carry the latter! No matter how clear a stream may appear, there is always the chance of pollution higher up the hill by animals. There is even the possibility of a dead one lying in the stream, as we have experienced on Dartmoor.

We are not considering climbing in this book, but for hill walking a light rope can be useful for linking members of the party if visibility gets very bad.

Route planning

Preparing a route card should be an essential part of your planning for a hill walk. In open hilly country away from villages the main hazards, apart from weather conditions, are likely to be caused by rough ground, cliffs, potholes and old mine workings. Watch out for these and take extra care. If your route is along a beach, check on the times of high tide; many beaches are completely covered, especially at times of spring tide, and it is all too easy to get marooned. Waiting several hours in discomfort before being able to continue is the least that could happen.

Before you start

If the weather is bad or likely to deteriorate within the next few hours, the wisest course of action is to postpone or abandon your walk. It may be possible to choose an alternative route avoiding high ground and open country. To make such a decision takes some courage if a walk has been planned ahead and you and your companions have been looking forward to it, but no-one with experience of the hills would criticise you for it. Some ideas on how to predict the likely weather situation are given in Chapter Five, but do take local advice. Although early morning mist in lowland and valleys can precede a fine day, mist on hilltops can indicate a very different story, leading to low cloud on high ground which can be very dangerous.

When you start, leave a note of your route, with starting time and estimated time of arrival at your destination and the number of people in the party. This can be left with, for example, a Youth Hostel warden, campsite warden, National Park information centre or even stuck in the window of your car if you leave it parked near the start. If for any reason you do not arrive at the expected place and time, it will be useful information for any rescue operations which may be set up later. It is, of course, equally important for you to report your safe arrival to wherever you left the information. Many hostels, campsites and information centres in popular hilly areas have a recognised system for receiving and acting on such information.

On the way

When walking with a small group, the leader should be ahead, with a responsible adult at the rear as backmarker. Both should have maps and compasses, and both should have the details of the proposed route in the form of a route card. Maintain a steady walking speed as far as possible, based on the speed of the slowest in the party, and don't start off with a rush!

Keep a frequent check on your position, using the map and compass and noting landmarks along the way. If a point on your route or a prominent landmark does not appear when you expect it, depending on time, position and distance travelled, stop. Re-check your route and position and try to pin-point exactly where you are. If necessary, backtrack to a known position and start again, or if conditions allow, regain your planned route as soon as possible, check, and continue.

If the weather conditions begin to deteriorate and visibility gets worse, immediately take note of your present position and check compass bearings ahead along your route. You may have to decide whether to continue, to return the way you have come, or to divert off your planned route and follow an alternative route, previously noted on your route card, to more sheltered terrain. It is possible you may encounter National Park Rangers – they can be a very helpful source of information about the route ahead and conditions, both weather and ground. Heed their advice, based on their local knowledge and experience.

Should visibility get so bad that you cannot see ahead for any great distance, consider using the rope to link the party together, and try sending one member ahead on the compass bearing, keeping just in sight, and correct his heading by checking with your own compass. Use this technique to leap-frog along until you are able to pick up visible marks far enough ahead. In these conditions you may have to make use of the method of 'aiming off' to a 'line feature', as described in Chapter Three, taking care always that you do not find yourself heading for the edge of a cliff, a steep rocky slope, or other hazard.

In very bad conditions of visibility, wind and rain, or even snow, it may be prudent to stop. Get all members of the party together, find a sheltered spot in the lee of bushes or rocks, put on extra warm clothing, and sit on waterproof sheets or insulating mats. Maybe a hot drink is called for while waiting for conditions to improve. If the conditions look set to continue so long that you will not be able to reach safer ground before dusk, consider pitching camp for the night if you have the necessary gear. Alternatively, get everyone into bivvy bags or survival bags, with warm clothes on, and prepare to stick it out until the morning, keeping warm with hot drinks and emergency rations.

Finally, when you are able to continue, either to your planned destination or to an alternative one reached after a diversion, don't forget to notify your safe arrival to those holding details of your trip.

Thunder storms and lightning

Thunder storms can be very frightening when you get caught out in the country, but there are simple precautions which can reduce the risk of being struck by lightning. Strikes tend to occur on hilltops and other projections above the surroundings, and the electric currents flow down gullies and across gaps under overhanging rocks. If a storm is approaching, move down from exposed ridges or tops, and find a position near a prominent feature such as a rock at least 10m high. A safe area extends to about the same distance as the height around the feature. Find a spot within this area but about 3 to 4 metres from the wall of the feature, and sit down on your sleeping pad or sit-mat with your knees tucked up and your hands in your lap. The object is to have as little contact with the ground as possible. Do not seek shelter in shallow caves or hollows, or in cracks or gullies, as these may form channels for rain water and will provide paths for the electric currents. If caught out in woodland, shelter below trees which are much lower than the surrounding ones. If these positions are not possible you are better off in the open, preferably on a scree slope, sitting on something dry as above, making as little contact with the ground as possible. Avoid isolated trees and wire fences. There is some evidence to suggest that beech trees are less likely to be struck than oak trees. Hail is often associated with thunderstorms.

Camping safely

The main hazards relating to camping are those associated with the use of stoves, lamps and when cooking. Any stove is as safe as the person using it, so make sure you understand the instructions for use, and always think of what you are doing.

The golden rule must always be never to change a gas cartridge or refuel a stove or lamp when it is hot, and always take it well away from the tent and from any naked flame or anyone smoking before loosening the cartridge or opening the fuel container. It goes without saying that the stove must be out before refuelling, but methylated spirit burns with a very pale blue flame which is almost invisible in sunny conditions. To check if your stove is really out, hold your hand high above it. If you cannot feel heat, try lower to make sure. Always turn off the control valve before doing anything else, and watch out for flaring when re-lighting after a cartridge change. Any apparently empty gas cartridge will still have a trace of gas inside, so place it well away from any source of flame.

Do not cook inside the tent. If the weather is bad, place the stove just inside

Tent pegs ensure the stove is safely set on the ground so it can't tip over

the entrance to the tent porch but do not obstruct your exit. It is safer to light liquid fuel stoves outside, if possible, because of flaring. Some stoves tend to flare when turning them off, so be prepared. Keep gas or liquid fuel lamps well away from the tent roof, preferably outside in the porch, and don't keep gas stoves and lamps inside the inner tent at night when you are asleep; a slight leak of gas can build up inside the tray groundsheet as the gas is heavier than air, and although not poisonous it can restrict the oxygen you need to breathe. When cooking, use a windshield. This will concentrate the heat and protect the flame from draughts which can cause flaring. Make sure the stove is stable on the ground and see that any pan is well balanced. One potential danger is caused by knocking the handle of a hot pan, so we recommend using pans with detachable gripper handles. If you are pitched among long grass, lay a piece of aluminium kitchen foil on the ground under the stove, and stand hot pans on a similar piece of foil. During the cooking operation, beware of splashing hot liquid or fat onto your skin. Finally, if the worst should happen and the stove flares up, grab it at the bottom and throw it well away from the tent if you can. Otherwise, get out quickly, which is where a second entrance is useful.

Dealing with emergencies

Getting help

If for any reason you require help, the recognised signal is six blasts on a whistle, followed by a wait of one minute, then repeat the six blasts. Continue until a reply is received. At night the same signal sequence can be made with a torch. If no whistle is available, wave a piece of cloth or other material in the same way.

The acknowledgement is three blasts or waves or flashes, followed by a one minute pause, then repeat.

If you see or hear a distress signal, immediately take a bearing on it before acknowledging it, then move towards the position. The signals should be repeated until the two parties are within sight of each other.

If distress signals bring no response or if you think it will be quicker to send for help, two people, if possible, should go, leaving at least one person with whoever needs help. Contact the police or a Mountain Rescue Post, giving the exact position of the incident with Grid Reference if possible, the nature of the incident, the number of casualties and their injuries in the case of an accident, and the time of the incident. These details should be written down before leaving the scene of the incident.

The people remaining at the scene should make their position as conspicuous as possible with improvised flags, bright clothing, etc.

Priority action

In any situation involving injury or illness the immediate priorities, before anything else, are to restart and maintain breathing, control any bleeding, and deal correctly with any loss of consciousness; at the same time, steps must be taken to protect the patient from any immediate danger. After that, what you do will depend on your knowledge as a first-aider, but the urgent need is to prevent any further risk to the patient while sending for help as described above. Keep the injured or sick person warm and comfortable, do not move, but provide shelter as quickly as possible.

Exposure

The medical term for this condition is Hypothermia, and it is brought on by a drop in the core temperature of the body. A tired walker carrying a heavy pack, soaked by rain, and exposed to strong winds with an air temperature below 8°C is a potential victim, so exposure need not be confined to hill walkers in winter. In summer, walkers are less likely to be prepared for the effects of wet cold. In fact we have seen an incipient case in a young camper in Kent who failed to take care of himself. In severe cases, death can result.

The usual symptoms may include pallor and shivering, slowing of physical and mental responses, general apathy, slurred speech, abnormal vision such as difficulty in focussing, irrational or violent behaviour, and unco-ordinated movement and eventual collapse. These symptoms may not all be present, and they will develop as the condition worsens.

It is important to observe one's companions and to note any changes such as the above, because the potential victim will not usually be aware of the onset, and collapse may occur within one to two hours. *Prevention* involves having warm clothing, including headgear, and putting it on in good time. Fully waterproof outer clothing should be used if the walk is to continue in rain. Wet cold kills! Fatigue, anxiety, insufficient energy-rich food and exposure to wind chill are contributory factors.

Immediate treatment is aimed at preventing further heat loss. Unless warmth and shelter is only a few minutes away it is essential to STOP, provide some sort of shelter on the spot and treat the patient by getting him into a plastic bivvy or survival bag then into a sleeping bag, well insulated from the ground by a sleeping mat or blankets, and sheltered from the wind and rain. Attempts to remove wet clothing will probably result in more heat loss, which must be avoided. Hot drink and food may be given, and other members of the party should provide shelter and warmth by huddling round, and have at least half an hour's rest before making any move.

Further action. Do not rush to continue the journey, and keep an eye on other members of the party for early signs of the condition. If satisfied of the patient's recovery, relieve him of his load and take the quickest and easiest route to shelter. If there is any doubt about recovery, make better shelter by pitching a tent or by rigging wind-breaks with whatever is available. Do not attempt to warm the skin by rubbing or by applying heat. Watch the patient carefully for any deterioration in his condition.

Get him to curl up inside the sleeping bag, and if possible someone can get into it with him to provide extra body warmth. Send for help as soon as possible but don't move the patient out of the warm 'nest' you have created. Hot sweet drinks and food can be given. Never give alcohol. Remember that exposure, if ignored, can lead to a serious life-threatening condition.

Snake bite

Snake bites are very uncommon in the United Kingdom, where we have only one poisonous snake, the adder. Its habitat is usually on heathland, bracken and dry grassland, and sometimes in the dunes in coastal areas. If adders are prevalent, there may be notices telling you to watch out for them. They will not normally harm you if left undisturbed, and if you make a lot of noise with your feet when walking through such areas they will slither away and hide. Should the worst happen and someone is bitten you must know what to do. Immediately you suspect someone has been bitten by an adder, lay them down and keep them as quiet as possible. Keep the upper part of the body raised slightly, so that the wounded part is kept below the heart level. Send someone to the nearest habitation to dial 999 for an ambulance, and tell them it is a case of adder bite. Since most bites will be on the legs, tie both legs together, thus supporting the injured limb. Do not tie a tourniquet around the limb, or cut the wound, or try and suck out the venom, but you can wash the wound with soap and water, if this is available.

Heart attack

This is another situation where keeping a watch on one's companions may prevent a serious situation developing. Symptoms may include any combination of the following:

Persistent violent chest pain spreading to the jaw and left arm

Shortness of breath

Weak or irregular pulse

Pale, grey, sweaty appearance

Nausea

Patient feels very frightened (or complains of indigestion)

Sudden collapse

Immediate action is aimed at reducing the work the heart has to do, by not moving the patient unnecessarily, and by placing him in the most comfortable position. This will probably be sitting or semi-recumbent, ideally on the ground leaning against a support, with the knees bent. Do not lie the patient down. Loosen clothing around the neck, chest and waist and encourage the patient to breathe deeply. Do not give any food or drink. Send for help immediately and watch carefully for any deterioration or stoppage of breathing and/or pulse. Be prepared to give resuscitation if necessary.

Swarming bees

You may think this an unlikely occurrence but we have seen a swarm in the Ashdown Forest, and have warned an approaching group of cyclists of the hazard. We have mentioned how to deal with bee stings in Chapter Six, but remember that a sting in the mouth can be serious and the patient should be taken to hospital as soon as possible (or telephone 999).

Swarming bees are usually harmless unless provoked. Stay still, do not run around or wave your arms. Move slowly indoors or into undergrowth, as this will confuse the bees, who prefer sunlight to shade. They aim for high points such as the head or hair, so crouch down and cover your head and face with your arms. Try not to kill any as this will anger the rest of the swarm, making them more likely to attack. Do not throw water over the bees, and if someone else is being stung, cover your face and move slowly to try and get them away from danger.

CHAPTER EIGHT

TAKING THE CHILDREN

Kitting them out

Basic kit

Most children start walking in the summer months, when the weather is fine and warm, and you will not have to worry about specialist gear for them. They will be quite happy walking in cotton T-shirts and shorts, wearing ordinary socks and shoes or well-fitting sandals on their feet. Sandals should not be of the 'flip-flop' or open toe variety, as they give no support to the feet and stones can get in too easily. Children also need a waterproof in case it rains, and a spare jumper for when they stop walking and it gets chilly, and it is a good idea to provide them with a small rucksack in which to carry their own things. Even quite small children are able to carry a 'fun' sack. It will be up to you to decide when they need to put on protective clothing; children do not always feel the cold until it is too late, and younger ones who are being carried or pushed in a buggy will not be moving sufficiently to keep warm. It is therefore very important to ensure they are properly clad, and that you carry sufficient extra clothing for them.

The same applies when taking small children cycling. When they are pedalling for themselves they will soon warm up, but if they stop pedalling, as they will when on a Trailerbike or the back of a tandem, then they will chill very quickly. Even more important is to ensure that children carried on cycle seats are protected from cold winds, although some protection will obviously be given by the adult on the saddle in front of them!

Choosing clothes

Children are very happy to wear 'carbon copies' of mum's or dad's clothes! Miniature fleece garments, cagoules and overtrousers are made by several quality manufacturers. Unfortunately, children's garments take as much time to make, or even more, as adult ones, and the cost is relatively high. As any parent will know, children grow rapidly, and if you have several children it can be expensive kitting them out, although it will of course be possible to hand down outgrown gear to the younger ones. One answer is to make the kit that you need for them; specialist, quality materials are available by mail order, as are patterns for waterproofs and warm clothing.

Children's waterproofs made by Yoredale Weatherware (Yoredale)

Underwear

Most of the high street stores make good underwear for children, both cotton and, increasingly, polyester or viscose. Some even make 'thermals' for children, and these are worth looking for. A reliable source of such garments is the Damart company, who supply either by mail order or from their own high street stores. Small children who are still in nappies need to be catered for. Always take extra disposable nappies, plus spare plastic pants, with you, even on a morning or afternoon outing. A child who suddenly becomes chilled is likely to have wet pants! Be prepared for this eventuality, even with older toddlers who may 'officially' be toilet trained.

Midwear

A T-shirt in warm weather, and a knitted jumper or warm sweat shirt in colder weather, are very suitable garments for children. They are bound to get dirty at some point in the day, and clothes that are easy to wash are obviously best. Track type or jogging trousers are comfortable and easy to get on and off, so are ideal. In cold weather, a fleece top and trousers are a better choice. These are made by, amongst others, Karrimor and Troll, and you may also find them in High Street stores. Prices will vary enormously. Fleece can also be obtained by the metre in various weights by mail order, and suits are easy to make, using a track suit pattern as a guide. Very small children, aged two and under, may be more comfortable in a one-piece suit. These are easily obtainable from babycare shops such as Mothercare, and the better High Street chain stores, or again, you can easily make one at home from a lightweight fleece fabric.

Shell clothing

In this category we should look at both windproof and waterproof clothing for children. Whilst a windproof garment might be considered an option for an adult, it makes sense to provide one for your children. Those who are being carried will need the extra protection when it is dry, but chilly. Older children will find the bright colours of the fabrics attractive, apart from the functional use of such garments. Because they are very light in weight, it is no hardship for children to carry them when not being worn.

Rainwear is very important. Very small children are best kept dry in a one-piece suit, and if they are prone to splashing around in puddles or crawling on muddy or wet ground these provide the perfect protection! Those being carried in a child-carrier can be protected by a specially made Papoose cover. Most stores now sell waterproof cagoules or jackets for children to wear to school – the days of school raincoats have virtually disappeared, and in any case these were quite ineffective in heavy rain. Do make sure that the garment you buy is big enough to go on over warm clothing, and that it is long enough. The hood should be elasticated round the face and should be attached to the garment so that it does not get lost. The cuffs should also be elasticated, or have built-in storm cuffs to keep out the rain. Drawcords at the neck and face are illegal on children's garments, although they are permitted at the hemline, if required. Provide your child with a pair of waterproof overtrousers as well, and he will be kept dry in very wet weather. Specially made children's gaiters, which older children may prefer, are made by Yoredale, who also make a wide range of children's waterproofs, including one-piece suits for very small children and the Papoose covers mentioned above.

Heads, hands and feet

A sun hat with a wide brim in hot weather and a woollen hat in cold weather are both essential. A warm scarf for those being carried on cycle seats or in child carriers is also necessary in winter. Gloves prevent hands from getting chapped in cold winds. Mittens are best as they are easy to put on, and can be made from wool, fleece, or even sheepskin. Attach them to a long tape threaded through the arms of your child's jacket so they do not get lost. To make sure your children's feet are warm enough, particularly when they are being carried, get them some woollen socks if possible. An old pair of dad's socks, with the feet cut off, pulled on over shoes and the bottoms of their legs will help keep the feet warm.

Footwear

Tinies who are being carried can safely wear wellingtons, provided they are not so large that they fall off in transit! When they do want to run around, wellingtons will at least keep their feet dry. Young walkers, from around the age of three, will probably be happy in ordinary lace-up shoes or trainers, but these, unfortunately, will not keep their feet totally dry. The answer is to treat the shoes with one of the specialist waterproofing products available from Grangers or Nikwax so that they are waterproof. What you use depends on whether the shoes are leather, fabric, or a mixture of both! In very wet conditions it might be an idea to let them wear their wellington boots, provided that they wear warm thick socks inside. It will be difficult to find walking boots for children of this age, so some compromise will be needed.

If older children are going to enjoy long walks in the countryside, they will have to be well shod. A pair of ordinary lace-up school shoes or trainers will be fine in the summer months, but in early or late season, and when there is a lot of mud around, they will be much happier in proper walking boots. Fortunately, these can now be obtained in high street and specialist stores, some, even those with a bellows tongue, costing no more than a good pair of shoes. Children's boots are normally available from about size 10, and although you should allow a bit for growth, do not get them too big or they will harm growing feet as much as those which are too small. The same basic principles apply to fitting children's boots as to adults; when the boot is unlaced and the foot pushed well forward you should just be able to get your finger down the back of the heel. We suggest putting a child into two pairs of comfortable socks before trying on a pair of boots, but no more than this. Towelling sports socks are available in children's sizes, and will be quite useful if you cannot obtain loopstitch socks for children, although these are available from about size 12 in specialist shops. Perhaps a willing Grandma would be prepared to knit walking socks for your children?

Carrying their kit

Children should be encouraged, from an early age, to carry their own things in a rucksack. Most outdoor shops and some chain stores and mail-order catalogues sell 'fun sacks' in the shape of animals which will be big enough to hold a small person's pullover and waterproofs. As they get older, buy them a proper daysack, with a capacity of 20 to 25 litres, and this will last, if taken care of, for many years. Shoulder slings should be made of good quality webbing that will not twist easily, and there should be plenty of adjustment. Most small day sacks do not have padded shoulder slings or hip belts, but a few are provided with a narrow waist belt. Packs which have two or three external pockets are more useful than those with none at all.

Older children should be able to carry all they need for the day, including their own packed lunch and drink bottle, spare clothing and waterproofs, plus 'I spy' or nature-identification books, etc.

The Macpac 'Possum' is an excellent example of a baby carrier. (Ian Gibson)

Children who cycle on their parent's tandem, in a child seat or on a Trailerbike will have their gear carried on the cycle with their parent's things. Those who ride their own bikes should be provided with a small saddlebag in which to carry their own gear.

Aids for walking

Don't be put off going into the countryside because your child is too young to walk. Tiny babies can be carried in a fabric sling, worn on the front of the body and tied at the back. These are obtainable at good baby shops. Excellent baby-carriers are now available to carry children from the age of a few months to four years, although one hopes they will be able to walk reasonable distances by the time they reach that age. Some carriers fold completely flat and have no supporting metal frame, whilst others are similar to a canvas bucket seat on a rucksack frame. Most, but not all of them, have a pocket in which you can stow spare nappies, Papoose cover, etc. One very interesting one, imported from New Zealand, has a 25 litre bottom compartment under the child's seat, giving plenty of capacity for the carrier's lunch, etc, as well as the passenger's needs!

If you have more than one small child, it can be a problem transporting them, but a 'buggy' can be pushed quite easily on grass and on firm paths, and can be folded to be lifted over stiles if necessary. The important thing is to encourage your young child to walk, even if only for short distances. Try playing an 'I spy' game, spotting trees and flowers, farm animals, etc. Carry a book which will help you identify some of the things you will see; if you don't know about trees and flowers, learn with your children, who may even be able to teach you a thing or two. It is surprising how much small children can learn.

Get the children interested in map reading

As your children get older, let them hold the map, secure in a transparent case, and show them where they are. This is not difficult if you show them whilst you are standing by a church or some other prominent feature which is actually marked on the map. You can also point to a feature in the distance which is also marked, and tell them that is where they are going, but don't do this when you are too far away or you could put them off! By the time they are seven years old, if they are reasonably intelligent, they should be able to read simple map signs and relate them to the things they see around them. By the time they get to nine years old, think about teaching them the rudiments of using a compass. We taught both our girls to use a compass before they were ten. When our younger daughter was nine, she had a go at walking on a bearing on a very misty day on Dartmoor. We were walking from the old Gidleigh Youth Hostel over the moors to Bellever. Having selected her bearing and checked it with us, we let her lead us across the moor, tied to the end of a long piece of guyline so that we did not lose her, because visibility was less than twenty yards! Half an hour later we reached the fence she was aiming for, right by the gate we needed. You don't have to go into wild country to teach your children, as they can easily learn on open common land or heathland, on the downs, or even in the local park. All these activities should be considered as aids to walking. If children's minds are occupied, they will forget their feet might be aching a bit in their eagerness to find out what comes next.

And babies came too! Walking a green lane in the Peak District the easy way. (Ian Gibson)

Aids for cyclists

There are more aids for cyclists to take the children out with them than there are for walkers. There are good children's seats available which fit on the rear of a cycle, usually to the seat stays and seat tube. You can also get seats to fit on the crossbar, although these are not so common. Always go to a specialist cycle shop for child seats, and whatever seat you get make sure there are firm fixing points for a harness to keep your child strapped in. Some seats come complete with a built-in harness. Ensure the seat is so designed that it is impossible for your child to get his feet caught in the wheel, and that there is also sufficient back and head support for very young children. When child seats are fitted it is not usually possible for panniers to be carried on the rear wheel, although you might get away with a small pair. Always make sure that children have plenty of waterproofing underneath them, as spray from the road can get through gaps in the seat moulding and get a child rather wet and muddy. A mudguard fitted to your cycle will help prevent spray getting to the child.

Travelling in style – a well designed child's seat on the back of a bike. (Chris Juden)

We recently saw a family out cycling with one of the adults riding a Pashley adult tricycle, with two small children in rear-facing seats on the back. Under the seats was a tray for luggage (or it could have been the shopping!) Both children were smiling and looked quite happy, but neither child was wearing a helmet, and we thought they looked rather vulnerable.

We do not recommend putting children under the age of 6 months into a child's seat on a cycle, but suggest they travel in a small trailer, specially made for the purpose. Most of these trailers accomodate two children side by side, and at the same time there is ample room for the day's requirements to be carried. Such trailers are expensive but they will be worth every penny if you plan to do a lot of cycling with a young family.

As children get older they will get great fun if they are given a Trailerbike, which is attached to the rear of an adult cycle. The child can pedal at his own rate, and can stop pedalling if tired. They are suitable for children from about the age of four to eleven, and they remain under your control whilst riding. They are easily detached if you want to use your solo bike between family outings.

Riding on the back of a tandem can also be fun, and children from three or four years of age are able to do this if the tandem is fitted with kiddy-cranks. These are linked to the rear drive mechanism of the tandem and have their own freewheel, so that the child can stop pedalling if he gets tired. Most of the work will be done by the adult in front, but at least the child feels he is making a contribution. Once a child is able to ride his own bike, introduce him gradually to the distances you wish to go. He won't be able to travel as far when solo as when he was on a Trailerbike or tandem!

Out with the family – riding on the back of a tandem can be fun. (Chris Juden)

Planning the trip

It pays to take special care when you are going out with children. Most half-day trips will be well within their capabilities, but when out for the whole day you have to be prepared to take it at your children's pace. You cannot hurry them along beyond their capabilities. The trick is to take them out little and often, increasing the length of your walk or ride each time, gradually building up their level of fitness and their ability to keep going. Frequent rests are needed, particularly when walking, and when cycling you have to be prepared for a child to get off his cycle when it becomes too hilly and push. It follows that you will have to get off too, and walk up the hill with him, although older brothers and sisters might be able to carry on with the other parent and wait at the top for you to catch up.

Do not be too ambitious; stick to short, easy walks and rides until your child becomes accustomed to the activity. Plan the route carefully, with the aid of a guide book, and get the children involved. Let them decide, with guidance, what they will need to take with them, and let them pack their own day sacks. Let them know how far they will have to walk before they get to their lunch stop, and let them see that there are interesting places to visit on the way there. If you are choosing a route of your own, and not using a guide book, plan carefully so that where possible ascents are less frequent than descents, and, when cycling, try to avoid a head wind. Look for a route that will offer the children plenty to see, including good views, and if you plan to stop at a pub it is worth checking, if at all possible, that there is a children's room or a dining room, where they can legally be taken. Nothing is worse than having to leave your children outside the pub with crisps and coke while you have a pint inside. Children need to rest, and sit down if possible, after a morning's ride or walk. It is worth looking to see if any National Trust properties are on the route; these often have a tea room where light refreshments are available, as do many garden centres. Such places are particularly useful for cyclists. Having said all that, perhaps it is safer to carry a packed lunch, and select several possible sites for a picnic when planning the route!

A five mile cycle ride or a two mile walk is quite enough for some children, so don't overstretch them or you might put them off. With encouragement and the right gear, they'll enjoy the activities to which you have introduced them. Once you have got them used to day trips, you can plan some weekends away with them, perhaps staying at a Youth Hostel or Bed and Breakfast. Even very small children will enjoy lightweight camping, provided that you stick to routine as much as possible, although they must have proper sleeping gear so that they are warm enough at night.

Safety for children

Whatever you do, you need to ensure the safety of your children. Teach them not to wander off, and not to go with strangers – elementary, but sadly children do forget this vital point. Use one of the wrist bands and cords that are available to keep children attached to you. Old-fashioned reins are coming back into use, and you can use them as a harness in a child seat. Attach a long strap to them so the child can feel freedom when running around, but is safe. Small children should be held by the hand when crossing roads, and when cycling keep them between two adults and ride in single file.

Ensure the children wear properly fitting helmets which will protect their heads if they fall off their bikes and fit their cycles with little plastic flags on a long 'aerial', which can be clearly seen by other traffic. If you use a trailer for your child, a 'baby on board' sign makes sense. Make sure children can control their bikes and ride in safety before you take them out on the roads, and teach them the Highway Code as soon as they are able to learn it.

When cooking in camp, you can ensure that a very small child or toddler cannot get near to a lighted stove by tying a length of guyline to the child's reins and pegging the other end to the ground

Take care, too, with countryside hazards, such as pools and streams, poisonous plants, and stinging insects.

In hot weather, protect your childrens' skin with protective cream, and ensure they wear a sun hat. Small children have a habit of pulling off their hats, so attach tapes to them and tie them on. Children also need to drink 'little and often' on hot days. Above all, teach your children to respect the countryside, and as they grow older, give them some books to identify the things that could harm them, so they can learn for themselves what is and is not safe to touch. They will enjoy their days out far more if they can learn that nature offers us all a variety of good things to eat and pretty things that can only be looked at.

CHAPTER NINE

EXTENDED JOURNEYS

The time will come when you or your family will not be satisfied with half-day or day-long walks or rides, and will want to take several days to explore one particular area. This is when you have to decide on your options. Will you go Youth-Hostelling, or take pot luck with Bed and Breakfast? Do you prefer to be totally independant and make the decision to carry your camping kit with you? The choice depends, to a certain extent, on how old your children are, if you are taking them with you, and how much you can afford to pay for your lodging for the night. It will also depend on where you are planning to go, because in some areas of the country Youth Hostels are very thin on the ground. In others there may be a shortage of Bed and Breakfast accommodation, or perhaps camping facilities may be limited. It may be that a combination of the first two may be needed, or possibly the option of mixing all three, but we will consider each in their turn.

Planning

Before you start on an extended trip, planning as described in Chapter Four will take on added importance. Your route must take into account where you will stop each night, and this will depend on what accomodation you plan to use. Another factor might be where you can shop for food on the way.

The estimated times and distances suggested for a day trip in Chapter Four may be too much to achieve when walking or riding for several consecutive days. It pays to plan for an 'easy' day, or even a 'rest day' every two or three days, depending on the conditions. This may allow you to do some sight-seeing, or even do some essential 'chores' such as washing clothes, checking over your kit, or doing a bit of maintenance on your bike.

Whether you prepare route cards for each day before starting out, or take this job on a 'one day at a time' basis is up to you – perhaps it would make a pleasant task after your evening meal, thinking about the next day's pleasures to come!

Youth Hostelling

The YHA is a registered charity, founded in 1930, with the aim "to help all, especially young people of limited means, to a greater knowledge, love and care of the countryside, particularly by providing hostels or other simple accommodation for them in their travels." Since its foundation, the YHA has expanded and now provides hostels ranging from the very simple to the (almost) luxurious, and membership is open to all age groups. Membership subscriptions and overnight charges vary according to age and the facilities offered by the particular hostel at which you stay, but children are enrolled free of charge when their parents are members. Hostels provide a solid roof over your head with beds, each equipped with a duvet or blankets and pillow, normally in single sex dormitories.

Youth Hostelling is a very good option for families, provided that the children have reached the age of five years. Children between the ages of five and thirteen can stay at a Youth Hostel if they are supervised by their parents or a responsible adult over the age of eighteen. A few hostels have self-contained family annexes accessible during the daytime for those with under fives, and some hostels can provide special family rooms. You should always check with the hostel warden in advance if you want to take small children with you.

The advantage of Youth Hostelling is that it is relatively cheap, and in most cases you can cook your own meals in a special members' kitchen where simple basic equipment is provided. The wardens often have a small stock of tinned food available for purchase, sufficient to provide a basic meal. To help keep their charges to the minimum, wardens may ask visitors to assist with simple chores, and most people are quite happy to do these jobs. You will be able to keep the weight of your luggage down, as you need only carry your overnight clothes, wash kit and towel, plus spare clothes, waterproofs, and soft shoes or slippers. It is a hostel rule that outdoor shoes or boots are removed before going indoors. Hostellers must use either a sheet sleeping bag to approved pattern, which can be hired at the hostel, or two sheets and a pillow case. You meet many different people from all over the world when hostelling in the U.K. You learn from them the good places to visit, as well as those which have not lived up to expectations! We have even walked into a Youth Hostel and met long-standing friends from overseas; both of us knew we would be touring in the area, but at different times, and had decided that, due to various commitments, it would be impossible to meet. Both of us changed our itineraries at the last minute, without the others knowing, and just happened to turn up at the same Youth Hostel! With the current difficulties over public transport in many parts of the country, particularly at weekends, hostels make a good base from which to start a few days walking, as you can sometimes arrange to leave your car at the first hostel you visit, and collect it at the end of your trip. Alternatively, you can use one hostel as a base, going out in a different direction each day.

Cyclists have the advantage of secure and covered storage for their cycles at Youth Hostels, although they should always lock their bikes with their own padlocks as well as securing the cycle-shed doors. Again, you will meet many cyclists on their travels who may be able to warn you of unexpected difficulties with bad road surfaces, etc.

You can often obtain a packed lunch from the hostel warden, as well as a good breakfast and evening meal if you do not wish to cook your own. Many hostels now have a cafeteria service, giving greater choice. Although hostel food is reasonably priced, it will be cheaper for you to take your own. On the other hand, if you have hostel meals you do not have to carry additional food!

It is wise to book all your accommodation before setting out, particularly if you are taking the family and in high season.

Bed and Breakfast

Bed and Breakfast provides a good alternative for those who want a solid roof over their head and a comfortable bed for the night, but who do not wish to share dormitory accommodation with strangers.

Tourist offices in the area you wish to visit can usually supply a list, sometimes free, and sometimes for a small charge. Both the Ramblers' Association and the Cyclists' Touring Club also publish accommodation lists. Some simple 'B and Bs' cost little more than hostel accommodation, although the more luxurious ones will obviously cost more. At a Bed and Breakfast establishment you will not be asked to help with the dusting or the washing up! Using this accommodation means you'll need to carry just basic overnight gear; take a hand towel with you, as these are not always provided. Some establishments, particularly in popular walking areas, are often able to provide packed lunches at a reasonable cost, but it is no hardship to carry the makings with you. Whether you are hostelling or using Bed and Breakfast houses, try to keep your kit within sensible proportions, and do not carry too much.

A useful checklist will be found in Chapter Ten.

Do not forget to take sufficient money with you, plus a cheque book. Credit Cards are accepted by some, but not all Youth Hostels, and Bed and Breakfast establishments usually prefer cash. Remember that cash machines are not very prevalent in the countryside!

Packing your kit

Walkers should make sure that their rucksack is large enough for the contents. It is best to choose one with an internal frame or semi-rigid stiffening, and one with a capacity of around 40 to 65 litres will be found ideal for hostelling purposes. It should have a well-fitting lid which covers the sack when full, so that no rain can get inside. Some sacks have a snow-lock or waterproof sleeve sewn to the top, which can be closed with a drawcord and gives total protection under the hood. Pockets also need well-fitting lids, and an inside pocket is useful for personal documents. Make sure the slings are fully adjustable and properly padded, and that there is a hip belt to allow the load to be transferred from your shoulders to your hips.

Pack the things you may need on your journey, such as your spare pullover and waterproofs, and soft shoes if hostelling, near the top of the sack, together with your lunch box and camera. First Aid kit and drink bottle can be packed in the rucksack pockets. Spare clothes should go at the bottom of the sack, with night clothes and toilet kit nearer the top.

Cyclists should carry their gear in a large saddle bag and/or panniers, not in a rucksack on their back. A cycle lock and an adequate tool kit should always be carried in addition to the items in our checklist in Chapter Ten.

Whether walking or cycling, pack all clothes in plastic bags to make sure they do not get wet.

Camping barns

In the last ten years various authorities have sponsored the conversion of a number of traditional barns into simple overnight accommodation. Often referred to as 'stone tents', they offer basic shelter for the night with a sleeping platform, cold water, tables and benches for eating and preparing food, and a toilet. You provide your own camping equipment, but of course you do not have to carry a tent. Some barns are a little more luxurious, providing showers and cookers, and therefore cost more than others. A few even provide beds and are more like simple Youth Hostels. All barns have to be booked in advance – you cannot just 'turn up', and since the sleeping arrangements are communal there is little privacy. They could be useful for family use, or for a group of friends walking together. Further details on how to book a camping barn will be found in Chapter Ten.

Backpacking

Some people prefer to be totally independant and carry their own shelter, so that they can be completely flexible and travel at their leisure, with no accommodation deadline to meet.

For walkers this means backpacking, carrying all you need during the day, camping for the night, and moving on again next day. Everything you needed for hostelling will be required, plus a good lightweight tent, sleeping bag and insulating mat, stove, pans, mug and cutlery, plus quite a bit of your food, especially if there are not too many shops where you are going.

Carrying your kit

Your choice of rucksack must depend on performance and comfort, as well as the size of your bank account. A rucksack with a capacity of 60 to 75 litres is recommended. Try to get one in which you can pack everything; dangling mugs and pans on the outside look untidy, and there is also the risk of getting tangled with branches and losing them.

Design of your pack.

The objective is to find a sack which will enable you to carry all you require with ease and in comfort. If you are not comfortable, then you will not enjoy backpacking. If your pack is not properly designed and the load is distributed wrongly, your natural reaction will be to compensate for the discomfort by walking with your back bent over to try and balance the load. This will result in uneven stressing on the discs between the vertebrae of your spine, possibly causing permanent damage. If, however, the discs are evenly stressed, they are capable of carrying a heavy load without ill effects; this is achieved by allowing the load to bear directly down the spine, which remains in an upright position. Modern sacks are designed with internal frames or flexible bars which can be shaped to fit the back, linked to carefully designed shoulder slings and hip belts which allow seventy per cent of the load carried to be transferred from the shoulders to the hips. This reduces fatigue because the shoulder and abdominal muscles are more relaxed. The load is carried close to the centre line of the body and allows the wearer to walk with the spine in an upright position, improving balance when walking or climbing over rough ground. It is important to ensure that the shoulder straps are wide enough and padded to prevent them cutting into your shoulders, but they should be tapered where they pass under the arms to the lower attachment points. The hip belt should also be firm and well padded, and be properly shaped to fit over the hips. It should be easily adjustable when fastened, and have some kind of quick release buckle so that your pack can be thrown off in an emergency.

You need to decide whether or not you want lots of pockets and a divided pack or one with a single large compartment. Most modern sacks are available with the main compartment divided in two by a removable divider, so it is easier to make your choice. There are advantages to both systems, the single compartment giving greater flexibility in packing. Some sacks incorporate extendable hoods and expanding side pockets, giving extra capacity when required, whilst others have the option of add-on pockets and accessory straps for carrying extra kit securely on the outside of the pack. Whatever sack you get, try to get one which is made from durable materials, as it can take a lot of knocks. Most rucksacks are made from heavyweight nylon with a waterproof coating on the inside, and often a water-repellant treatment on the outer. Special fabrics may be used for the backs of sacks to help combat sweating, which is bound to occur when the sack is close to your back. These can take up a certain amount of water, but also dry quickly.

Fitting your pack

The comfort of your pack is dependent on the correct fit. A well-fitting pack allows the load to be balanced between the shoulder harness and the hip belt without putting a strain on your shoulders and arms. The size of the frame must suit the length of your back, or you'll be very uncomfortable. Even on a weekend trip the wrong back length can make a big difference to your comfort. Some sacks are available in different back lengths, whilst others can be adjusted to fit within a certain size range. Many of those with an adjustable back system, but not all, can be adjusted while the pack is being worn.

The only way to assess how comfortable a pack will be in use is to try it on with sufficient weight inside. An empty rucksack will never feel the same as one which is full, and you should have an idea of your estimated load before buying. A good specialist retailer will be happy to load a pack with weighty items to help you choose. Some rucksacks are available in ladies fittings, with specially shaped shoulder slings and hip belts. These are well worth looking for. There is no substitute for a personal fitting by the trained, experienced staff of a specialist retailer, but if you have to order through the post choose a pack with an adjustable back system and buy from a specialist mail order company who will advise on fitting and be prepared to exchange your pack if it does not fit. As a general rule, the centre point on the shoulder harness, where it is attached to the frame, should be level with the centre of your shoulder blades, and the hip belt should fit snugly on the hips and not round the waist. To get an idea of your correct back sizing, get a friend to measure between the prominent bone at the base of the neck to a point level with the top of your hip bones. Add about ten centimetres (four inches) to this measurement, and you will have a good idea of the length of frame required. Fine adjustment is possible on most frames by using 'lift straps' or top tension straps on the shoulder slings. Sometimes a chest strap is fitted, which helps control the position of the shoulder straps, and is very useful if you have narrow shoulders.

Packing your sack

To ensure that your load is positioned on your back so that the weight acts in a line directly down through the spine to your feet on the ground, you need to keep the centre of gravity of that load as high and as near to the centre of your back as possible. The heaviest items should be placed near the top of the pack, adjacent to your back. However, heavy items tend to be large and sometimes awkwardly shaped, so some compromise is often required. You may prefer to pack heavy things down the length of the pack, closest to your back, and the lightest things away from your back, with the rest sandwiched in between. We prefer to put the lightest things at the bottom of the sack, medium weight things next and the heaviest on top. So, the sleeping bag goes in first, followed by the sleeping mat.

Spare clothes are packed in the small spaces around these items before the washing kit, pans and food go in. The tent goes on top, together with the waterproofs and spare pullover. The stove and gas cartridges (or fuel bottles) go in one outer pocket, and the first aid kit in another. Although rucksack materials are, in theory, waterproof, it is always safer to use a large polythene bin liner inside the sack, and pack individual items in polythene bags. You will have to find the best way to suit you, dependent on the size and bulk of your kit, but the principles remain the same. Never pack an empty space, so make sure your cooking pans are filled with some of your food.

Cycle camping

When cycle camping you will be carrying your kit on your cycle, and will need to get used to doing so before going on a trip. Take your time and adjust to the new feel of your cycle, and remember that it will take you longer to stop when you apply the brakes. Remember too that you will go downhill much faster with a heavy load, so take extra care on steep hills and where there are sharp bends.

Carrying the kit

The same things will be needed for cycle camping as for backpacking, except of course for the rucksack. Never, ever carry a rucksack on your back when cycling, as it will affect the balance and control of your machine. On the bike, kit will be packed in panniers, with perhaps a saddle bag and front bar bag. Water, drinks and liquid fuel for a stove can be carried in bottles in cages fastened to the down tubes of the cycle frame.

Pannier frames

Panniers should be firmly attached to a proper pannier carrier so that they cannot swing about. If you are also using a saddle bag you might need a bag support, especially if your saddle is adjusted to a fairly low position. Some people prefer to spread the load over both wheels, and in this case you also need front panniers and a front carrier. 'Low loading' frames for the front wheels are a good idea, but do not overload the front of the cycle or the steering can become affected.

Purchase your pannier carriers from a proper cycle shop and get them fitted properly. Good carriers are strong, light in weight and rigid. They must be fixed so that there is no risk of their coming loose when loaded or on the move. There should be proper fixing points for the base of the panniers, and provision for fitting a cycle lamp to both front and rear carriers, as the normal fitting point may be obscured by the panniers.

Full camping kit should be well distributed for balance on a bike

Cycle bags

Most modern cycle bags are made from similar materials to backpacking sacks – strong, proofed nylon fabrics which will withstand a lot of wear. It is still possible to obtain canvas panniers, although most of the nylon bags have a greater capacity. Remember that cycle bags are subject to a lot of abrasion where they come into contact with parts of the cycle frame, so they should be well reinforced at these points. Some means of stiffening is necessary to keep the sides of the panniers which are closest to the wheel rigid. Separate rear pannier bags are more convenient in a tent than those which are linked together and slung across the carrier, but it is useful if they can be linked with a strap or other device to assist carrying when off the cycle, and to give additional security when on it. Front panniers are usually smaller, and if the front carrier is not a 'low loader' a pair which is joined by a bridge of fabric is not too much trouble. However, it has to be said that separate panniers are much more convenient. Rear panniers are usually tapered towards the front, so that they do not foul the heels of the cyclist. Most have a good sized rear pocket, and some have an additional pocket on the front panel. Saddle bags need to be roomy, and front bar-bags have to be properly supported so that they do not interfere with the brake and gear cables. It is most important that all cycle bags have really good closures to keep out the rain, and all zips should be well protected. Upward splashes of water from the road, plus wind accentuated by the movement of the cycle can cause problems.

Packing your kit

When packing kit on a cycle, keep the weight as low as possible – the opposite, in fact, from packing a rucksack. It must also be distributed evenly, so that the weight in each opposing pannier is about equal. You will still have awkward loads to pack, especially if you have a budget tent with rather long poles! Distribute the load so that about two thirds is over the rear wheels and the rest over the front wheel. Do not overload the front bar bag, but keep it for personal items and use as a shoulder bag or handbag when sightseeing. Pack your cycle tools in one of the pannier pockets or in the side pocket of your saddle bag. These need to be accessible without opening the main bag, and of course they are rather dirty items and need to be kept separate. If your sleeping bag is very bulky, it may fit inside a large saddlebag, especially if you use compression straps. Another idea is to line one rear pannier with a large bin liner and stuff the sleeping bag straight into it, pushing it well into all the corners. Pack all your spare clothes into the second pannier, together with your toilet kit and a light pair of spare shoes, and the balance should be about right. Pack all clothing and bedding items in plastic bags or waterproof stuff sacks so that there is no chance of them getting wet. Your stove and cooking pans, food, etc, can be packed in the front panniers, and the tent and rolled sleeping mat can be securely fastened across the back carrier. Tent poles can be strapped to the cross bar if they are too long to go elsewhere, but should be in a bag and securely fastened on.

Packing for the family

When packing the kit for cycling, and you have young children on cycle seats on the bike, you can carry slightly more in the front panniers, especially if they are 'low loaders', but only if the child on the back is around three years old and has a reasonable body weight. The front load must still be one third of the rear. If it is impossible to fit panniers under the child's seat, then consider getting a small luggage trailer. For families riding tandems, you still have the problem of carrying two persons' kit on two wheels instead of four, but by using large panniers at the rear and 'universal' (small rear panniers) on the front wheels, plus a large saddlebag, you should be able to manage. A trailer on a tandem is not very practical, although we have seen one in use.

Choosing your camping kit

Shelter for the night

A good lightweight tent will be your most expensive piece of kit but it is your home for the time you are away. When choosing it, bear in mind that you may find yourself having to sit out some pretty foul weather if you are unlucky. The usual material for a good backpacking or cycle camping tent is polyurethane-proofed ripstop nylon for the outer flysheet, and either woven nylon or cotton for the inner tent, to allow warm moist air to escape. Otherwise, condensation will form inside.

Aim for a tent that weighs about two kilograms (four and a half pounds) per person using it. Some quite good budget-priced models are obtainable, although they will be a little heavier and the materials may be of lower quality. There are some well-designed tunnel or hoop tents, sloping ridge and transverse ridge tents within this category which all pack small enough to be carried in a rucksack or on a cycle. Go for a tent which can be pitched flysheet first, so that you can get shelter quickly and get your kit under cover if the weather turns nasty. We recommend a transverse ridge or tunnel tent with two bell ends for families, so that cooking can be done at one end and the children given access at the other. If you are cycle camping take particular note of the packed size, and try to choose one with a maximum packed length of 50cm. If necessary, poles can be taken out of the main bag and carried in a separate bag securely fastened to the cycle.

Sleeping well

You need to keep warm at night, so a good sleeping bag is essential. There are many man-made fibres which will keep you warm, but some can be very bulky and difficult to pack, although compression straps can help to keep the size down. Less bulky man made fibres also tend to be more expensive, but ongoing developments offer improvements almost every year. If you can afford it, a down filled sleeping bag will pack smaller that others, and will last a very long time if cared for. The one drawback is that down is useless as an insulator if it becomes wet. The best type of bag is a mummy shape, tapered to the feet and with a hood to draw up round the head in cold weather to prevent heat loss. A zip may be fitted to the side for ease of entry, and it is possible to buy bags in pairs to zip together. Childrens' tapered bags are also available. A double layer or shingle construction bag or wall-quilted down bag is better than a 'stitched through' bag, as there will be no cold spots. (Figure 9.1) A hostel-type sheet sleeping bag, used as a liner, will help keep your bag clean.

Good insulation under your bag against cold rising from the ground is essential. The cheapest is a closed cell foam mat, but this can be a bit hard. The modern self-inflating mats, filled with a softer foam and air, are much more comfortable and warmer. Air beds are heavy and do not give sufficient insulation.

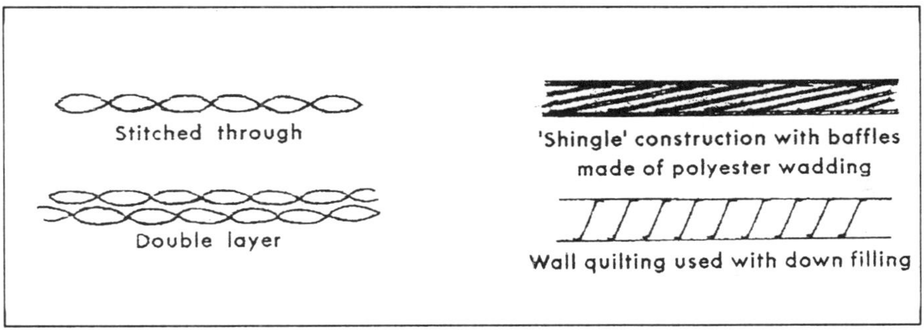

Figure 9.1. Sleeping bag construction

Stoves and pans

It follows that if you are camping you are going to have to cook your own food, but a heavy stove is not needed. The best type to use is one which folds very small, but is stable when opened out and stood on the ground. The choice of stove depends partly on personal preference and partly on availability of fuel. Gas (technically known as Liquid Petroleum Gas or LPG) in disposable cartridges is convenient, and for colder times of the year the best is a mixture of butane and propane which is readily available. We have no hesitation in recommending self-sealing screw-on cartridges which conform to the Standard EN 417 in preference to pierceable cartridges, on grounds of safety and convenience. Gas stoves can be low-profile burners connected to the cartridge by hose, or burners which screw directly onto the cartridge. A windshield is an almost essential requirement and the cartridge and stove can be pegged to the ground to prevent them from falling over.

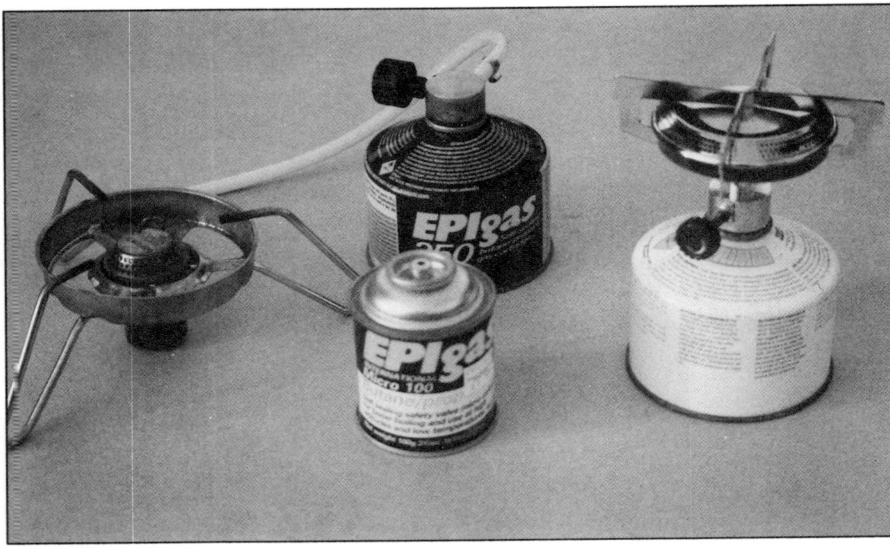

Some lightweight gas stoves. Epigas 'Alpine' (left) and Primus 'Weekender' (right) use resealable cartridges

Liquid fuel pressure stoves are very efficient in all conditions. Of the fuels available, paraffin is probably cheapest but requires pre-heating when lighting the stove. Petrol is used in several very efficient stoves, but some people do not like the fumes and feel unsafe with such a volatile liquid. Unleaded petrol as used in cars can be used but may cause clogging of the burner jets. Petrol stoves operate well on Coleman Fuel, an additive-free grade of petrol for camping use which is rather expensive.

Methylated spirit is used in several types of non-pressurised camping stove, the best known being the Trangia which is sold as a complete cooking set, including windshield, pans and a kettle.

With any of the liquid fuels, suitable containers are needed, and it is good practice to wrap the fuel bottles in plastic bags and always carry them in the same pocket of the rucksack or cycle bag in case of leakage.

Cooking pans of aluminium are light to carry, but avoid if you can those which are very thin – the food will burn easily. Recently, aluminium pans with a stainless steel lining are becoming available, also some good sets with non-stick surfaces. We do not like pans with attached handles as they are often unstable and it is easy to burn the hands on the handle. Detachable grip handles are safer to use.

The Optimus Mini-Camper burns paraffin and the Trangia cooking set uses methylated spirit

Food

Whatever you cook will use fuel, so try to avoid foods which require a long cooking time. In some areas, water can be in short supply and you will need to carry sufficient for basic needs, so there won't be any to spare for making up dehydrated foods. In any case, some of the dehydrated meals on the market require two or even three pans and up to 30 minutes cooking time. It pays to study the cooking instructions on the packet before buying! Some ready-made meals are available, specially made for backpackers which, although perhaps a little heavy, are ready to use and do not need gallons of water to reconstitute them. Of course, if you are going to use a camp site, you will not have problems with water.

We normally carry a ready-made meal each for emergencies, plus dry foods like savoury rice, pasta, instant soups, dried milk, instant whips, etc. We usually carry one or two small tins of meat to form the main protein content of our meals. Cheese is a useful standby, and can be grated before leaving home. If you pass a village shop or one of the many garage shops now appearing you can often stock up with a frozen meal en route to your night halt. Long life meals are also very good, but check that you do not need a microwave oven to cook them! Many can be heated in a pan of hot water, which can double as washing-up water or even for making a hot drink. Tips like this can save you a lot of bother. A lot depends on your own personal tastes, but you will not want to be weighed down with too much tinned food or have to carry a lot of water.

Some bits and pieces

There are always those little things which seem to get left behind. Even if your gas stove has piezo-ignition, don't forget some matches, carried in a watertight tin. Cruet and a corkscrew, not to mention the tin opener, and a pair of folding scissors (not those in the first aid kit) are invaluable for opening food sachets or cartons of long life milk which never work the way the instructions say!

You will need some light in the tent at night, but a battery torch is safer than candles and lighter to carry than any of the gas or petrol lamps on the market. If cycle camping, you have the ideal tent light, namely your front battery lamp, but do carry spare batteries. Another useful type of lamp is a headlamp with internal batteries, useful when pitching in the dark and for cooking at night.

CHAPTER TEN

HELPING YOURSELF

Information

In this chapter we give you some useful information about different organisations which may be of help to you, as well as addresses where you can find out about accomodation and equipment. In addition, we include some rules to help you and others to enjoy the countryside, and suggest some check lists which may help you when packing your kit. We also give some hints on caring for your gear, and a list of helpful magazines. For convenience, all the relevant addresses are listed *en bloc* at the end of the chapter.

Useful Clubs to join

Having kitted yourself out for walking or cycling in all weathers, and probably spent a considerable amount of money in doing so, it follows that you will want to make the best of using your equipment. One way is to join a club which caters for your particular interest. For walkers, the Ramblers' Association has many local groups which meet regularly for social evenings and organised rambles in their local area. You automatically become a member of your local group and are sent contact information when you join. Members receive a quarterly magazine called Rambling Today, as well as a free copy of the Ramblers' Yearbook and Accomodation Guide. There are, of course, many other local rambling clubs relating to particular areas, and details of these can usually be found in your nearest public library. Cyclists can do no better than join the Cyclists' Touring Club, which also has local groups and District Associations (D.A.s) who hold regular meetings and organise cycle runs for both fast and slow riders. Some groups also arrange cycle camping weekends. All CTC members receive a bi-monthly magazine, Cycle Touring and Campaigning, plus a copy of the CTC handbook. The Youth Hostels Association is an obvious choice for both walkers and cyclists, particularly those who like to be out during the winter months and want to make the maximum use of the daylight hours available. A regular magazine, Triangle, is sent to members, who may also obtain the YHA Accomodation Guide free of charge. There are YHA local groups throughout the country, who meet for social evenings and arrange hostelling weekends and other walking and cycling activities for members. There are separate Youth Hostel Associations for Scotland and Northern Ireland.

Both backpackers and cycle campers are welcome in the Camping and Caravanning Club, which produces two excellent sites books, plus a monthly magazine, all exclusive to members. Many of the Club's 'D.A.s' arrange rambles from their weekend camping meets, and also Saturday or Sunday rambles during the winter months. This club was founded by cycle campers at the turn of the century, and today has a special section for lightweight campers. Club members may join the Association of Lightweight Campers for a small extra subscription, and are kept in touch with like-minded members through a quarterly magazine. There is also a Mountain Activities Section, catering for campers of all kinds who enjoy the sort of activities discussed in this book. Like the Association of Lightweight Campers, a small extra fee is charged and members also receive a quarterly magazine.

All the above named clubs have a paid Headquarters staff, but local District Associations, Groups and Sections are run entirely by volunteers. The Backpackers' Club is a relatively small club of dedicated individuals who organise informal backpacking weekends, mostly during the winter months. The Club produces its own magazine and Farm Pitch Directory, available only to members. All local co-ordinators are volunteers, and there is no paid office staff.

Other useful organisations

The National Trust owns many beautiful areas of countryside, some of which are more than big enough to offer scope for a day's walking, and sometimes more than this. For example, much of the South West Coast path is owned and managed by the Trust. There are also many fine properties to which members have free access. Many of these have tea rooms which make useful stops on a walk or cycle ride if you plan your journey carefully, but unfortunately most are only open between Easter and October, and close during the winter months. The Trust also publishes many leaflets on country walks, relating to their properties.

Overnight accomodation

In Chapter nine we suggested various places to stay overnight on longer journeys. If you are not a member of the Ramblers' Association you can purchase the annual Ramblers' Yearbook and Accomodation Guide direct from them for around £5, plus £1 for postage. It may also be obtained from most larger branches of W.H. Smith. The Cyclists' Touring Club's Handbook and Accomodation Guide is also available to non-members for £2.15 (1995 price). The YHA Accomodation Guide is obtainable through branches of W.H.Smith. If you are not a member of the Camping and Caravanning Club or the Backpackers' Club, campsite information is available from the relevant local Tourist Information office. Camping barns are owned by the farmers on whose land they are situated, but most are normally booked through area reservation offices. The Youth Hostels Association publishes three leaflets giving information about a network of camping barns in the Forest of Bowland, the North Pennines and in North Yorkshire. The booking address is different for each area. The Peak District National Park also has a leaflet available, and organises the booking of all the camping barns in the Peak District. The Yorkshire Dales National Park publishes a list of Bunkhouse Barns (with more facilities than a basic camping barn), plus a few camping barns. The addresses for booking the accomodation are given, but may not be those where the barn is actually situated. The National Park Authority point out that the inclusion of a bunkhouse or barn on their list should not be taken to imply any guarantee of standards, nor that the statutory requirements such as those in respect of public health, fire certification etc. have necessarily been met. The National Trust lists one camping barn (Gumber Bothy, near Slindon, West Sussex), in the National Trust Handbook. However, they also own a number of Base Camps, which are normally used by their volunteer groups. A few of these may be used for recreational purposes and some can be booked by individuals and/or groups. Most offer dormitory accomodation, showers and toilets, plus cooking facilities. A booklet giving information on Base Camps is available from the Volunteers Office in Cirencester.

Tourist Information Offices in the main centres will be able to provide a list of Bed and Breakfast establishments, and may also be able to book accomodation for you. National Park Offices can also help with information about the area to which you are going, many of them providing useful leaflets about the countryside attractions, plus information on local walks. Some may also have accomodation lists. Addresses of all the National Park Offices are given at the end of this chapter.

Kit by mail

Most people will be able to find a good supplier of walking and camping kit in their nearest large town, where a good cycle shop can usually be found as well. If you live a long way from such places, there are several reliable mail order suppliers who can help. These include Field and Trek, Cotswold Camping, Culverhouse, The Adventure Centre, and Wilderness Direct. All have a good range of clothing, boots and rucksacks as well as lightweight tents, stoves and other camping equipment, and most of them list children's clothing. Field and Trek and Cotswold Camping also carry a range of cycle clothing, panniers and carriers. For cyclists who have no access to a local specialist shop, the CTC can supply a number of items, including panniers and clothing, by mail order. If you are not a member, we suggest you send for the current copy of 'Cycle Touring and Campaigning', costing £1.75 (1995 price), which always carries a large number of detailed advertisements from specialist suppliers.

Insurance for your kit

It is worth checking that your equipment is covered by reliable insurance, particularly if you are camping. Many household policies will offer extensions to cover your camping kit and possessions when away from home, but it is wise to check that your own insurers will do so. Most clubs offer third party insurance cover as part of their membership package, and can offer other specialised insurance cover at attractive rates.

The Country Code

When you are in the countryside you should observe this general code of behaviour published by the Countryside Commission.

- ❒ Enjoy the countryside and respect its life and work.
- ❒ Guard against all risk of fire.
- ❒ Fasten all gates.
- ❒ Keep your dogs under close control.
- ❒ Keep to public footpaths across farmland.
- ❒ Use gates and stiles to cross fences, hedges and walls.
- ❒ Leave livestock, crops and machinery alone.
- ❒ Take your litter home.
- ❒ Help to keep all water clean.
- ❒ Protect wildlife, plants and trees.
- ❒ Take special care on country roads.
- ❒ Make no unnecessary noise.

The Offroad Cycling Code

The following code has been drawn up by the British Mountain Bike Federation for the guidance of offroad cyclists in the countryside.

1. Stay on the trail
   Only ride bridleways and byways.
   Avoid footpaths
   Plan your route in advance
   Use the Pathfinder/Landranger maps

2. Give way to horses and walkers
   Make sure they hear you approach
   Ride carefully when you pass

3. Bunching is harassing
   Ride in twos or threes

4. Be kind to birds, animals and plants
   And keep your dog under control

5. Prevent erosion
   Skids show poor skills

6. Close gates behind you
   Don't climb walls or force hedges

7. Stay mobile
   Wear a helmet
   Take a first aid kit
   Carry enough food and drink
   Pack waterproofs and warm clothes

8. Take pride in your bike
   Maintain before you leave
   Take essential spares and tools

9. Be tidy
   Take your litter home
   Guard against fire

10. Keep smiling
    Even if it hurts!

The Mountain Code

These guidelines have been prepared by the British Mountaineering Council, and contain good advice for those venturing into the hills, whether they are walkers or climbers.

- Be prepared
- Do not tackle anything which is beyond your training and experience.
- Ensure your equipment is sound.
- Know the rescue facilities available in the area you are in and the procedure in case of accidents.
- Know first aid.
- Avoid going into the mountains alone unless you are very experienced.
- Leave word of your route and proposed time of return.
- Always report your return.
- Make sure your map and compass skills are well practised. Rely on your compass.
- Consider other people
- Avoid game-shooting parties.
- Lead only climbs and walks which you are competent to lead.
- Enjoy the quiet of the countryside; loud voices and radios do disturb.
- Do not throw stones or dislodge boulders.
- Do not pollute water.
- Choose a climb which will not interfere with others, or wait your turn.
- Be weather wise
- Know the local weather forecast.
- Weather conditions change rapidly. Do not hesitate to turn back.
- Know the conditions on the mountain; if there is snow or ice only go out when you have mastered the use of ice axe and rope.
- Respect the land
- Keep to footpaths through farm and woodland. If in doubt, ask.
- Camp on official sites or obtain permission of the landowner.
- Dig a hole to make a latrine and replace the turf.
- Remember the danger of starting a fire.
- Take all your litter home.
- Avoid startling sheep or cattle.
- Help conserve wildlife
- Enjoy the plants, flowers and trees but never damage or remove them.
- Avoid disturbing wildlife.

Check lists

You will help yourself greatly if you make a check list of all the equipment you need to take with you, be it for a day's walking with the family or a week-long backpacking trip on your own. Obviously your needs will differ slightly if you are walking and camping with a friend, with whom you can share a tent, stove and pans than if you have to carry everything yourself. Make a separate list for each eventuality, and keep them where you will not lose them! Don't forget to add the children's things to your check list if they are too small to make their own. Some suggested check lists are given below.

Summer Day walk with children

- ❒ Day sack, plus 'fun sacks' or small sacks for children
- ❒ First Aid kit
- ❒ Waterproof jackets and overtrousers
- ❒ Spare pullovers or fleece tops
- ❒ Packed lunches
- ❒ Thermos of coffee or tea
- ❒ Soft drinks for children
- ❒ 'I Spy' guide
- ❒ Map and compass
- ❒ Camera
- ❒ Small waterproof 'sit-mats'
- ❒ Money for fares, etc.
- ❒ National Trust membership cards

For a summer day cycle ride you will need the same equipment, carried in a saddlebag or a pair of universal panniers.

The kit needed for hostelling on foot

Overnight Hostelling trip in Autumn

- ❒ Rucksack, 45 – 60 litre capacity or Pair rear cycle panniers or large saddle bag
- ❒ First aid kit
- ❒ Waterproof jacket and overtrousers
- ❒ Spare pullover or fleece top
- ❒ Spare underwear
- ❒ Warm hat and gloves
- ❒ Sheet sleeping bag
- ❒ Night clothes
- ❒ Soft shoes or slippers
- ❒ Washing kit and towel
- ❒ Spare shirt and trousers
- ❒ Spare socks
- ❒ Torch
- ❒ Map and compass

- ❐ Camera
- ❐ YHA membership card, National Trust card
- ❐ Money for fares and hostel fees
- ❐ Food for packed lunches and self-catering
- ❐ Thermos flask
- ❐ Spare Plastic bags – for lunch packs, packing wet things, etc.
- ❐ Cycle lock and tool kit (for cyclists only)

Week-long backpacking or cycle-camping trip with a companion

- ❐ Rucksack, 60 to 75 litre capacity, or pair of large rear panniers and pair of front panniers
- ❐ Lightweight tent (shared)
- ❐ Sleeping bag and sheet liner
- ❐ Sleeping mat
- ❐ Night clothes (spare tracksuit is ideal)
- ❐ Washing kit and towel
- ❐ First aid kit
- ❐ Waterproof jacket and overtrousers
- ❐ Warm hat and gloves
- ❐ Spare pullover or fleece top
- ❐ Spare underwear
- ❐ Spare shirt and trousers
- ❐ Spare socks (2 pairs)
- ❐ Gym shoes or light sandals
- ❐ Stove and fuel (shared)
- ❐ Cooking pans (shared)
- ❐ Water bottle/container (shared)
- ❐ Mug, plate, bowl and cutlery
- ❐ 2-litre ice cream box or similar, for wash bowl
- ❐ Torch and whistle
- ❐ Map and compass
- ❐ Camera
- ❐ Camping Club or Backpackers' Club membership card
- ❐ National Trust card

- ❒ Money for fares, camp site fees and food
- ❒ Food for two days minimum (shared)
- ❒ Emergency food
- ❒ Thermos flask
- ❒ Spare Plastic bags – for lunch packs, packing wet things, etc.

The cycle camper needs a tent among his kit

Looking after your kit

You have invested a lot of money in your equipment, so it will pay you to look after it well. Wash clothing carefully, following the manufacturer's instructions on the care label. Note that some 'thermal' and fleece fabrics should not be washed in very hot water or tumbled dry. Others, however, can be subjected to quite high temperatures and no harm will be done. Repair holes or tears in clothing as soon as possible to prevent further damage. Waterproof garments need treating with care, again following the care label on the garment. Most 'breathables' can be washed, but one of the special washing products from Nikwax or Grangers is recommended. Tumble drying is often recommended as it can help to regenerate the water repellancy of the outer fabric. Check with the care label on your garment. Coated, non-breathable waterproofs are best washed by hand, using a specialist product or pure soap flakes. They should be rinsed thoroughly with cool water and allowed to drip dry. Do not leave any wet or damp waterproof rolled up for a long time – always dry it off as soon as possible.

Boots and shoes need treating with a waterproofing compound, although when some boots are new they will need little, if any treatment, since the leathers are specially treated during manufacture.

Always wash dirty boots with cold water as soon as possible after use, to remove mud, etc. This is particularly important if you have been walking over peat or along the shoreline, as peat and sea sand can damage the leather and soles of your boots if not cleaned off. Once washed, allow the boots to dry naturally and *never, ever* in front of a fire, near a hot radiator or in a hot airing cupboard. Stuff wet boots with newspaper, and replace with fresh paper after a couple of hours. When boots are dry, treat with Nikwax or G-Wax, or one of the other special boot products from these companies. Some of the new water-based products from Nikwax can be applied to wet leather, which can be useful if your boots take a long time to dry!

Mud should be brushed off rucksacks and panniers with a medium-stiff brush when the mud is dry. Check periodically for worn straps on the harness, or broken buckles, and get them replaced. Zips which are jamming can sometimes be eased by rubbing a graphite pencil along the track.

Tents should be dried as soon as possible after returning home, and aired thoroughly before packing away in a dry place. Alloy tent poles can be kept in good condition by a light application of silicone polish, which helps prevent them jamming and assists against corrosion. Guylines and pegging loops should be inspected regularly, and broken ones replaced or repaired. Tent pegs should be washed and straightened, and lightly coated with silicone polish.

Sleeping bags should be thoroughly aired and loosely folded for storage. A floor cushion cover or large pillow case makes an ideal storage bag. Never store a sleeping bag in a polythene sack or transparent plastic storage case, as condensation can occur, causing mildew. If it is necessary to wash your bag, use a specialist product, especially if the bag has a down filling. If you have a sleeping bag dry-cleaned, it must be thoroughly aired in the open air for several hours to ensure all traces of fumes from the cleaning process are removed. We recommend, therefore, that sleeping bags are washed, and not dry cleaned.

Stoves should be regularly maintained and kept clean. Separate gas hoses should be checked and replaced after about three years. Sealing washers should be checked every time the stove is used to ensure they have not come adrift.

Finally, if you travel by cycle, always maintain it in good condition, and check regularly for loose nuts and bolts, particularly on carrier frames and mudguards.

Addresses of Clubs and other organisations

The Ramblers' Association, 1/5 Wandsworth Road, London SW8 2XX Tel:0171-582-6878

The Cyclists' Touring Club, Cotterell House, 69 Meadrow, Godalming, Surrey GU7 3HS Tel: 01483-417217

The Youth Hostels Association (England and Wales) Trevelyan House, 8 St Stephen's Hill, St Albans, Herts AL1 2DY Tel: 01727-855215

Scottish Youth Hostels Association, 7 Glebe Crescent, Stirling FK8 2JA Tel: 01785-51181

Youth Hostels Association of Northern Ireland, 56 Bradbury Place, Belfast BT7 1RU Tel: 01232-324733

The Camping and Caravanning Club, Greenfields House, Westwood Way, Coventry CV4 8JH Tel: 01203-694995

The Association of Lightweight Campers, c/o The Camping and Caravanning Club (address as above)

The Camping and Caravanning Club Mountain Activities Section, Greenfields House (address as above)

The Backpackers' Club, PO Box 381, Reading, Berks RG3 4RL. Tel: 01491-628739

The National Trust, 36 Queen Anne's Gate, London SW1H 9AS. Tel: 0171-222-9251

Booking Camping Barns

Bowland Barns Reservation Office, 16 Shawbridge Street, Clitheroe, Lancs. BB7 1LY. Tel: 01200-28366 (24 hr)

North Pennine Barns, Langdon Beck Youth Hostel, Forest-in-Teesdale, Co. Durham DL12 0XN. Tel: 01833-22372 (24 hr)

North Yorks Barn Booking Office, YHA Northern Region, POBox 11, Matlock, Derbyshire DE4 2XA. Tel: 01629-825850 (24 hr)

Peak District Barns Booking Service, Losehill Hall, Castleton, Derbyshire S30 2WB Tel: 01433-620373

The Volunteers Office, National Trust, 33 Sheep Street, Cirencester, Glos. GL7 1QW. Tel: 01285-651818

Cycling Permits (Tow Paths)

British Waterways, Willow Grange, Church Road, Watford, Herts WD1 3QA. Tel: 01923-226422

National Park Offices

Brecon Beacons National Park, 7 Glamorgan Street, Brecon, Powys LD3 7DP. Tel:01874-624437

Dartmoor National Park, Parke, Haytor Road, Bovey Tracey, Devon TQ13 9JQ. Tel: 01626-832093

Exmoor National Park, Exmoor House, Dulverton, Somerset TA22 9HL. Tel:01398-23665

Lake District National Park, Murley Moss, Oxenholme Road, Kendal, Cumbria LA9 7RL. Tel: 01539-724555

Norfolk and Suffolk Broads, The Broads Authority, 18 Colegate Norwich, Norfolk NR3 1BQ. Tel: 01603-61073

North Yorks Moors National Park, The Old Vicarage, Bondgate, Helmsley, York YO6 6BP. Tel: 01439-70657

Northumberland National Park, Eastburn, South Park, Hexham, Northumberland NE46 1BS. Tel: 01434-605555

Peak District National Park, Aldern House, Baslow Road, Bakewell, Derbyshire DE45 1AE. Tel: 01629-814321

Pembrokeshire Coast National Park, County Offices, Haverfordwest, Dyfed SA61 1QZ. Tel: 01437-764591

Snowdonia National Park, Penrhyndeudraeth, Gwynedd LL 48 6LS. Tel: 01766-770274

Yorkshire Dales National Park, Colvend, Hebden Road, Skipton, North Yorks BD23 5LB. Tel 01756-752748

Mail Order Suppliers

Field and Trek Plc, 3 Wates Way, Brentwood, Essex CM15 9TB. Tel: 01277-233122

Cotswold Camping Ltd, Broadway Lane, South Cerney, Cirencester, Glos. GL7 5UQ. Tel: 01285-860612 (24 hr)

Culverhouse, 96 The Parade, Watford, Herts WD1 2AW. Tel: 01923 244100

The Adventure Centre, Evans House, Norman Street, off Orford Lane Warrington WA2 7HW. Tel: 01925-411385

Wilderness Direct, PO Box 49, Skipton, North Yorkshire BD23 2YY. Tel: 01756-796840 (24 hr)

Pennine Outdoor, Hard Knott, Holmbridge, Huddersfield, West Yorks HD7 1NT. Tel:01484-689100 (Specialist fabrics by mail order)

Useful Magazines

These magazines carry regular product information of interest to walkers, as well as walks information and routes: *Country Walking, Trail Walker, The Great Outdoors*. All are on sale in major newsagents, or can be ordered through your local newsagent.

For those with a particular interest in hill walking, *Climber and Hill Walker* will be of interest, and for backpackers and other campers *Camping* magazine may be of some help.

Other product information

Manufacturers and distributors will not normally supply direct to members of the public, but many will be happy to send you information about their products and advise of your nearest stockist. The following list of some of the major manufacturers and suppliers may be of help. The list is not exhaustive, and there are plenty of others. Inclusion of a manufacturer or supplier in this list does not necessarily mean recommendation or approval of all their products.

Key: C=Clothing, R = Rucksacks, B = Boots, Cy = Cycle equipment, Sl = Sleeping bags, St = Stoves, T = Tents

Berghaus Ltd, 17-19 Brindley Rd, Hertburn Industrial Estate, Washington, Tyne and Wear NE37 2SF (C,R,B.)

Burton McCall Ltd, 163 Parker Drive, Leicester LE4 0JP (C,R,B,Sl.)

Calange Outdoor Clothing, PO box 61, Stockport, Cheshire SK3 0AP (C)

Coleman UK Plc, Parish Wharf Estate, Harbour Road, Portishead, Bristol BS20 9DA (St, Sl)

Craghoppers Ltd, Bradford Road, Birstall, Batley, W.Yorks WF17 9DH (C)

Damart Thermawear Ltd, Bowling Green Mills, Bingley, West Yorks BD97 1AD (C)

db Mountainsport Ltd, 10 Kent Street Kendal, Cumbria LA9 4UA (C,B,R,T)

J.J.Hawley Ltd, Lichfield Road, Walsall, West Mids. WS4 2HX (T)

Karrimor International Ltd, Petre Road, Clayton-le-Moors, Accrington, Lancs BB5 5JP (C,R,B,Cy,St.)

Mountain Equipment, Peaco House, Dawson Street, Hyde, Cheshire SK14 1RD (C,Sl)

Sprayway Ltd, 16 Chester Street, Manchester M1 5GE (C)

Primus Ltd, Stephenson Way, Formby, Merseyside L37 8EQ (R,St,T)

Rab Down Equipment, 32 Edward Street, Sheffield S3 7GB (C,Sl)

Robert Saunders (Chigwell) Ltd, Five Oaks Lane, Chigwell, Essex IG7 4QP (C,T)

Snugpak, Waterloo Mills, Howden Road, Silsden, W.Yorks BD20 0HA (C,Sl)

I and M Steiner Ltd, Reynard Mills Trading Estate, Windmill Road, Brentwood, Brentford, TW8 9LY (R,Sl,T)

Taymar Ltd (Epigas), Wear Mill, King Street West, Stockport, Cheshire SK3 0AJ (St)

Vango (Scotland)Ltd, 70 East Hamilton Street, Ladyburn, Greenock PA 15 2UB (C,R,B,Sl,T)

VauDe (UK) Ltd, Unit DC 72/5, Haltwhistle Industrial Estate, Haltwhistle, Northumberland NE49 9HA (C,R,Cy,Sl,T)

Jack Wolfskin Ltd, 12A Kingtown Broadway, Carlisle, Cumbria CA3 0HA (C,R,Sl,T)

Yoredale Weatherwear Ltd, 1-3 Well Lane, Batley, WF17 5HQ (C)

Baby carriers

These are made or distributed by:

Dalesman International Ltd, Dalesman House, Marathon Place, Moss Side Industrial estate, Leyland, Lancs PR5 3QN and also by Calange, Karrimor, Vango and VauDe (addresses above)

The Macpac baby carrier is available from Cotswold Camping (address above)

Cycle seats for children

(Note: These are distributors or wholesalers, who will not normally supply direct to the public, but can tell you the name of your local retailer.)

Belvis UK Ltd, 59, Tallon Road, Hutton Industrial Estate, Brentwood, Essex CM13 1TG

Fisher of Finchley, Unit 2, Haslemere Busines Centre, Lincoln Way, Enfield, Middlesex EN1 1TE

Moore Large and Co, Grampian Buildings, Sin Fin Lane, Derby DE24 9GL

Newman Distributors, Oxleasow Road, East Moons Moat, Redditch Worcs B98 0RE

Raleigh Industries (Parts and Accessories Division) Triumph Road, Nottingham NG7 2DD

Children's Trailers, etc.

BLI Group, The Camel Trail, Wadebridge, Cornwall PL27 7AL

Roper and Co Ltd, 44 South Road, Erith, Kent DA8 3RA

Islabikes,252 Halesown Road, Cradley Heath, West Midlands B64 6NH (Trailerbikes)

W.R.Pashley Ltd, Masons Road, Stratford on Avon CV37 9NL (Tricycles with attached child seats)

Care and Maintenance

The following can supply information about care and maintenance products or services:

Grangers International Ltd, Grange Close, Clover Nook Industrial Park, Alfreton, Derbyshire DE 55 4QT

Nikwax Waterproofing, Unit F Durgates Industrial Estate Wadhurst, East Sussex TN5 6DF

Shoecare Ltd, Yarrow Mill, Yarrow Road, Chorley, Lancs PR6 0LP

Other useful addresses

Harveys, 12-16 Main Street, Doune, Perthshire FK16 6BJ

Ordnance Survey, Romsey Road, Maybush, Southampton SO9 4DH

Silva (UK) Ltd, Unit 10, Sky Business Park, Eversley Way, Egham, Surrey TW20 8RF

Index

D

E

F

Notes